Theology Today

GENERAL EDITOR

EDWARD YARNOLD, S.J.

No. 26

The Theology of Confirmation

BY

AUSTIN P. MILNER, O.P.

FIDES PUBLISHERS, INC.
NOTRE DAME, INDIANA

Nihil Obstat:
Jeremiah J. O'Sullivan, D.D.
Censor deputatus
30 June 1972

Imprimatur:
Cornelius Ep. Corcag. & Ross
21 July 1972

SBN 85342 292 3

ABBREVIATION

Dz: H. Denzinger & A. Schönmetzer, *Enchiridion Symbolorum, Definitionum et Declarationum* (33rd edit., Barcelona etc., 1965)

ACKNOWLEDGEMENTS

The Scripture quotations in this publication are from the Revised Standard Version of the Bible, copyrighted 1946 and 1952 by the Division of Christian Education of the National Council of the Churches of Christ in the U.S.A. and used by kind permission. Thanks are also due to the Clarendon Press for permission to quote from Dom Connolly's edition of the *Didascalia;* to the National Liturgical Commission of England and Wales for the use of their copyright translation of the Confirmation Service; and to the Newman Press, Westminster, Maryland, and to Longmans Green and Co., London, for permission to quote from *St. John Chrysostom: Baptismal Instructions,* ed. P. W. Harkins.

PREFACE

In recent years the meaning of the sacrament of confirmation has been keenly debated in the Catholic Church. Is it simply the last stage in the initiation of a Christian? Is its purpose to strengthen the Christian for the trials of adult life? Is it a 'sacrament of the lay-apostolate', by which a Christian receives the power of the Holy Spirit to enable him to spread the Gospel? Is it primarily an opportunity for a mature commitment to the Church? Anglicans, too, have found themselves divided in their interpretation of confirmation. These are not merely academic speculations; until the theological questions are answered, it is impossible to decide at what age the sacrament should be administered and how the candidates should be instructed.

The Apostolic Constitution of 1971, with its new rite of confirmation, goes some of the way towards giving us the answers. Fr Austin P. Milner's book might be seen as the theological and historical foundation of the Constitution. His magisterial presentation of the evidence will dispel a number of misconceptions. His linking of the two main patterns for confirmation in the early Church respectively with the Pauline and Lukan theologies of the Spirit is particularly illuminating and exciting.

E. J. Yarnold, S.J.

INTRODUCTION

There has been continuous controversy about the rite of confirmation for the last thirty years. The traditional theology has been challenged from two sides. For some it is a meaningless reduplication of an aspect of baptism; for others it is nothing less than the baptism in the Spirit promised by Christ for which water baptism is only the preparation. Although the literature of this controversy is large we are still without a satisfying theology of the sacrament. Historians are now in general agreement about the development of the rites, but they still dispute their interpretation. The theologians have not yet managed to assimilate the historical researches and still remain inordinately attached to the limited mediaeval view of the sacrament which rests on very dubious foundations. In such a situation the urgent pastoral problems concerning the age for receiving confirmation and the catechetics connected with it find no ready solution, and there is a tendency to use the sacrament as an opportunity for meeting pastoral needs which have little to do with it. The charismatic renewal among both Anglicans and Catholics has stimulated a new and vital interest in the working of the Holy Spirit in the Church, but those who look to the doctrine of confirmation for enlightenment in these matters find little to help them.

The task of writing a short book on the theology of confirmation in these circumstances is a difficult one. Theology is not history, yet the theology of Christian sacraments must be firmly based on the actual practice of the Church in different places throughout the centuries. The history of the Church's practice in this matter poses not a few problems for the theologian as does also the obscurity of its origins.

History, therefore, must feature largely in any book on the theology of confirmation. First of all we must outline the history of the gift of the Holy Spirit in the initiation rites of the early Church. Then attention must be given to the development of episcopal confirmation as a separate rite. Only after this will a fruitful discussion of the relevant New Testament texts and a theological treatment of the problems be possible.

CONTENTS

CHAPTER 1

THE GIFT OF THE SPIRIT IN THE EARLY RITES OF CHRISTIAN INITIATION

The texts of the New Testament, which may throw light on the conceptions of the primitive Church with regard to the reception of the Spirit and the fulfilment of Christ's promise in the rites of initiation, are so difficult to interpret that they are better left until we have studied the practice of the Church throughout its later history. Outside the New Testament our earliest information on the rite of baptism is found in the *Didache* but it contains no reference to the use of oil in the rite nor to any laying on of hands. About the year 150 St Justin Martyr gives in his First Apology a description of Christian initiation by baptism and participation in the eucharist, but again there is no reference to the use of oil nor to any laying on of hands. The argument from silence is always precarious, but had Justin been familiar with the use of oil or a laying on of hands for the invocation of the Holy Spirit either in Rome or anywhere else, it is difficult to think of any reason why he should not mention them. The conclusion that he knew nothing of such rites is strengthened by the remarks of St Irenaeus on a Gnostic sect called the Marcosians. These, he says, anoint the baptized with *myron* after the baptism, as a symbol of his 'good odour' before God. Some, he says, even substitute an anointing with oil and water for the baptismal immersion itself (*Adv. Haer.* I. xiv). It is clear from the author's tone that, even thirty years later than Justin, he is not familiar with any such practices among Catholics. Soon afterwards, however, at the beginning of the third century there is abundant evidence for the use both of oil and of hand-laying in Catholic initiation rites and it is hard to believe that

11

these practices were entirely unknown in the late second century. The most explicit evidence comes from the West, but for reasons which will become apparent it is more convenient to take the Eastern evidence first.

The Baptismal Rites of the Church of Antioch

The church of Antioch extended its influence over all the Christian communities westward through Cappadocia, Asia, and across to Macedonia and Achaia, eastward to Mesopotamia and beyond and southward along the coast of Palestine. It was far bigger and liturgically more influential than either the church of Alexandria or that of Rome, especially as from the fourth century it included in its sphere of influence the imperial city of Constantinople. The baptismal rites of this church are therefore of the greatest importance. Our earliest evidence concerning them comes from a document known as the *Didascalia Apostolorum,* dating from the first quarter of the third century. Baptism is mentioned only in connection with the appointment of deaconesses. These are said to be necessary because there are many matters in which the service of a woman deacon is required.

> In the first place, when women go down into the water, those who go down into the water ought to be anointed by a deaconess with the oil of anointing. And where there is no woman at hand, and especially no deaconess, he who baptizes must of necessity anoint her who is being baptized. But where there is a woman and especially a deaconess, it is not fitting that women should be seen by men. But with the imposition of the hand do thou anoint the head only. As of old the priests and kings were anointed in Israel, do thou in like manner, with the imposition of the hand, anoint the head of those who receive baptism, whether of men or women; and afterwards – whether thou

baptize thyself, or thou command the deacons or presbyters to baptize – let a woman deacon, as we have already said, anoint the woman. But let a man pronounce over them the invocation of the divine names in the water (Ed. Connolly, p. 146*f*.).

In this rite, therefore, there is an anointing of the head with laying on of the bishop's hand followed by an anointing of the whole body. This is followed by baptism and the invocation of the divine names. The anointing is associated with the anointing of priests and kings in Israel, so perhaps it was illustrative of the kingly and priestly dignity of the Christian in the sense of 1 Peter 2.

The same order of baptism is followed in all the accounts of baptism in the Syriac version of the apocryphal Acts of Judas Thomas which was written about the same time. Baptism is referred to as the seal by which God knows his sheep. The anointing is often accompanied by a prayer that the Lord may abide upon the oil. First the head is anointed, and then the whole body is anointed, women's bodies being anointed by women. The baptism in water follows and the ceremony ends with the Eucharist (Whitaker, pp. 10-13). The same order of anointing followed by baptism is found in the Clementine Recognitions (III, 67), a work which can be dated between 211 and 231. The next evidence for this rite occurs in the works of Ephraem in the middle of the fourth century. He too is familiar with an anointing before baptism: 'with chrism ye have been sealed, in baptism are ye perfected, in the flock are ye intermixed, from the body are ye nourished' (The Nicence & Post-Nicence Fathers (Second Series) XIII, p. 270).

At the end of the fourth century the same rite is described in detail and commented on at length by St John Chrysostom and Theodore of Mopsuestia (although, as we shall see later, Theodore also has a postbaptismal anointing); and in the following century by Proclus of Constantinople and Narsai of Nisibis. Theodoret of Cyrrhus (c. 393-

13

c. 458) seems to know of no other rite.

In all these later authors the ceremonies described are more complicated than those of the *Didascalia,* but the basic pattern remains unchanged as can be seen from the comparative table (p. 116f.). It is not so much the order of the rites which concerns us here as the interpretations put upon these different ceremonies.

The first rite, that of marking the sign of the cross on the forehead with *myron* or scented oil is rich in meaning. The Acts of Judas Thomas, Theodore of Mopsuestia, Ephraem and Narsai see it in the seal or brand set upon the sheep of Christ's flock. In the apocryphal Acts especially, prophylactic power is attributed to it; Chrysostom, Theodore and Narsai dwell upon the idea that the Devil cannot bear to look upon this mark of the cross; it protects them from him and gives them the right to look at Christ. This leads to the idea that the seal is the mark of the soldier of Christ's army which is found in all these commentaries, but the military analogy is particularly dear to Chrysostom who returns to it on many occasions. The signing with the cross marks out the candidate for spiritual combat; indeed it marks his entry into the arena. Sometimes for Narsai the arena is especially that of baptism itself; but for Chrysostom it is the whole of the Christian life, a combat with the Devil in which Christ is not only the judge but enters on the side of the Christian.

The anointing of the body is associated by the *Didascalia,* by Ephraem and Chrysostom with the kingly and priestly dignity of the Christian. For Theodore the covering of the whole body with oil is a sign that the candidate is about to be anointed with the robe of immortality by the baptism itself. Chrysostom and Narsai see in it a fortification of every bodily member against the Devil and the providing of spiritual arms for the combat. The Spirit, according to Narsai, gives power to the oil to confirm the candidate so that he may make war on evil.

14

Ephraem and Theodoret (*In Cant.* 1, 2) attribute the gift of the Spirit to this anointing but certainly not in any separation from baptism. Chrysostom, on the other hand is most insistent that the Holy Spirit descends upon the candidate at the very moment of baptism:

> After this anointing the priest makes you go down into the sacred waters, burying the old man and at the same time raising up the new, who is renewed in the image of the creator. It is at this moment that through the words and the hand of the priest [i.e. the bishop], the Holy Spirit descends upon you. Instead of the man who descended into the water, a different man comes forth, one who has wiped away the filth of his sins, one who has put off the old garment of sin and has put on the royal robe (Harkins, p. 52).

It is not possible to divide this rite of initiation, which we may call the Antiochene rite, into two sacraments, one corresponding to baptism, the other to confirmation as conceived in the West. Anyone wishing to do so must either postulate that the pre-baptismal anointing constitutes a confirmation before baptism – which is absurd, or he must say that the two sacraments are conferred simultaneously by the laying on of the bishop's hand in the baptismal act. It is simpler to understand that these writers of the church of the East did not know any distinction between a sacrament of baptism for the forgiveness of sins and rebirth, and another sacrament for the reception of the Spirit. There is, however, some evidence that the need for a rite by which the Spirit could be given was felt in this region by the last quarter of the fourth century. This we shall see later.

The Western Rites of Christian Initiation

We are fortunate enough to possess accurate and detailed descriptions of the rites of initiation in the West dating from

15

the beginning of the third century. The chief of these is the *Apostolic Tradition* of Hippolytus of Rome written about 213. According to this document the candidate is anointed with oil after the renunciation of Satan, but the oil is oil of exorcism and the meaning of the anointing is brought out by the words which accompany it: 'Let all evil spirits depart far from thee'. The triple immersion is accompanied by a triple interrogation of faith, while the bishop or presbyter lays his hand on the candidate's head.

> Afterward, when he comes up he shall be anointed with the oil of thanksgiving with these words: 'I anoint thee with holy oil in the name of Jesus Christ', and so, each one drying himself, they shall now put on their clothes, and after this let them enter the church. And the bishop shall lay his hands upon them invoking and saying:
>
> 'Lord God, who didst make these worthy of deserving the forgiveness of sins by the laver of regeneration, make them worthy to be filled with thy Holy Spirit and send upon them thy grace that they may serve thee according to thy will; to thee is glory, to the Father and to the Son with the Holy Spirit in the Holy Church both now and for ever and world without end. Amen.'
>
> After this, pouring the consecrated oil from his hand and laying it on his head he shall say: 'I anoint thee with holy oil in God the Father almighty and Jesus Christ and the Holy Spirit.' And sealing him on the forehead he shall give him the kiss of peace and say: 'The Lord be with you.' And he who has been sealed shall say: 'And with thy spirit.' And so shall he do to each one separately (ed. Botte p. 51-55; cf. Whitaker p. 6).

The first anointing before the baptism is a strengthening and protecting of the candidate for his confession of Christ in the baptismal act. The baptism is followed by two anointings. The minister of the first is not specified and we may take this to indicate that it may be a presbyter. No explanation is attached to it. The laying on of the hand with prayer, the further anointing and the signing which take place when the candidates are clothed, are to a large extent explained in the prayer which the bishop is directed to say. It is addressed to God who through baptism has already conferred on the candidates the remission of sin and the grace of regeneration. A further grace is now asked: that they may be filled with the Holy Spirit and receive grace to serve God according to his will. Clearly the author conceives this reception of the Holy Spirit as something different from the regeneration received in baptism. Elsewhere in the writings of Hippolytus 'the power of the Holy Spirit with which the believers are anointed after their washing as with chrism' is said to have been foreshadowed by the oil with which Susannah anointed herself after her bath (*In Daniel.* 1, 16,3). The sign of the cross with which the bishop marks the forehead is seen not only as the seal which identifies the believer as Christ's property, but also as the outward sign of the indwelling Spirit with which the believers are sealed (*De Antichr.* 59).

The preachers who used the Antiochene rite were not tempted to attribute to the prebaptismal anointings and signings effects which were different from and in addition to that of the baptism itself. The rite described by Hippolytus lends itself to just such interpretation, especially as, under the influence of the account in the Acts of the Apostles of the conversion of the Samaritans (ch. 8) and that of the disciples of John at Ephesus (ch. 19), it was easy to see a resemblance between the laying on of the bishop's hand after the baptism, and Peter and Paul laying their hands upon people already baptized. Is the rite described by Hippolytus dependent upon these accounts or only the interpretation it receives?

Tertullian's homily on baptism shows the dangers of this

17

kind of thought. He is speaking of the miracle at Bethesda as an example of what happens to the Christian in baptism, for there too an angel gave healing power to the waters. But the analogy must not be pressed too far: 'Not that the Holy Spirit is given to us in the water, but that in the water we are made clean by the action of the angel and are made ready for the Holy Spirit' (*De Bapt.* 6). The action of the angel is compared to that of John the Baptist making ready the paths for the coming of the Spirit. Sins must first be cancelled before the Spirit can come, and his coming is the effect of the laying on of the bishop's hand: 'At this point that most Holy Spirit willingly comes down from the Father upon bodies cleansed and blessed' (*De Bapt.* 8).

Tertullian's thought on this matter, however, is not clear. It is probably wrong to take this passage as witness that he made a sharp distinction between the negative effect of baptism and the positive gift of the Spirit as the effect of the hand-laying. He believes that 'in the water we are born anew according to Jesus Christ' (*De Bapt.* 1): in the water we are remoulded and fashioned anew (*De Bapt.* 3; *De Carn. Christ.* 17). What he wishes to affirm is that as we come out from the washing the Holy Spirit comes down upon bodies cleansed and blessed, as he came down upon Jesus at his baptism in the form of a dove, bringing to us the peace of God, as did the dove which flew back to Noah's ark. He has nothing to say about the charisms of the Spirit at this point, but at the end of the homily he exhorts his hearers as follows:

When you come up from that most sacred washing of the new birth, and when for the first time you spread out your hands with your brethren in your mother's house, ask of your Father, ask of your Lord, that special grants of grace and apportionments of spiritual gifts (*peculia gratiae distributiones charismatum*) be yours. 'Ask,' he says, 'and you will receive.' So now you have sought, and you have found: you have

18

knocked, and it has been opened to you (*De Bapt.* 20).

The rite which Tertullian was commenting upon, differed from that of Hippolytus chiefly in having only one post-baptismal anointing (see tables p. 118ff.). Tertullian does not connect this anointing with the gift of the Holy Spirit but with the baptism itself. He sees it as the consecration of the Christian: 'Flesh is anointed that the soul may be consecrated' (*De Res.* 8). He associates it with the anointing of Aaron and the priests of the Old Testament, and the fact that the Lord obtained his title, 'Christ', from his anointing with the Spirit by God the Father (*De Bapt.* 7).

The rite of Christian initiation used by St Cyprian of Carthage (d. 258) seems to have been very similar to that of Tertullian. Like Tertullian he distinguishes between the effects of baptism and those of hand-laying, though he does not think of the baptism simply in negative terms. The baptismal act produces the remission of sins, but it also entails being sanctified and spiritually re-made into a new man; it is nothing less than the putting on of Christ and becoming the temple of God. The actual reception of the Holy Spirit, the pouring out of the Holy Spirit upon the temple, is brought about by the laying on of the bishop's hand. (*Epist.* 74,5). The power of the Spirit is active in the baptism – for how else could these effects be brought about? – but the Spirit is not 'given' or 'received' except by the hand-laying. Cyprian tries to clarify this distinction by comparing baptism to the forming of Adam, and the reception of the Holy Spirit through hand-laying, to the breathing into him of the spirit of life. 'It is not possible to receive the Spirit unless he who receives already exists' (*Epist.* 74,6).

This distinction is reminiscent of one made by St. Irenaeus (bishop of Lyons 178-200) between two different functions of the Holy Spirit in the Church. He is responsible for forming us into one body with Christ as water unites the grains of flour which make the bread and congealed the

19

particles of dust from which Adam was moulded (*Adv. Haer*. III, 17). In this way the Holy Spirit establishes our nature as members of Christ. It is a process of unification, of sanctification and purification, which he compares to the action of the good Samaritan in binding up the wounds of the injured man *(ibid.)*. This function is distinguished from what he frequently calls 'giving to drink' after St Paul in 1 Corinthians 12.13: 'For by one Spirit we were all baptized into one body... and all were given to drink of the one Spirit' (*Adv. Haer*. III, 17,2; IV, 33,14; *Demonstr*. 89). To this latter function of the Spirit in the Church Irenaeus attaches great importance. In this activity Christ makes the believers share the anointing which he himself received (*Demonstr*. 47). It is manifested particularly through the gift of prophecy which, in fulfilment of the words of Joel, exists throughout the Church. Through this gift of prophecy man bears fruit to God, speaking before the world with boldness and thus drawing others into the mystery of salvation. Heretics cut themselves off from this operation of the Spirit, 'for where the Church is, there is the Spirit of God, and where the Spirit of God is, there is the Church and all grace' (*Adv. Haer*. III, 24,1; cf. III, 11,12; III, 17; *Demonstr*. 99). In the Church which Irenaeus knew all the charismatic gifts of the Spirit were in evidence.

> Those who are truly his disciples, and have received the grace from him, perform in his name the same miracles for the benefit of the rest of men, according as each has received the gift from him. For some cast out devils really and truly, so that those same persons who are purged of evil spirits often become believers and are in the Church. Others again have foreknowledge of things future, and visions, and prophetic sayings. Others heal the sick by the imposition of their hands and restore them whole. Before now, as we have said, dead persons have been raised and have stayed with us a good number of years. And what

shall I say? There is no numbering the gifts which in all the world the Church has received from God, and in the name of Jesus Christ, crucified under Pontius Pilate, exercises daily for the benefit of the nations, neither deceiving any nor stripping them of their money. For as she has freely received of God, so also she freely ministers (*Adv. Haer.* II, 32,3).

It is much more difficult to determine whether Irenaeus connected this second function of the Spirit with any particular rite. We have seen indications that he probably knew nothing of the use of oil in Catholic baptism. There are passages in which he seems to regard the operation of the Spirit as the inward counterpart of the baptismal washing (*Adv. Haer.* V, 11,2; *Demonstr.* 89); in others he seems to distinguish the effect of baptism from the gift of the Spirit. Thus he describes the apostles 'purifying their [the gentiles'] souls and their bodies through the baptism of water and the Spirit, dispensing and administering to the faithful the Holy Spirit they had received from the Lord' (*Demonstr.* 41). In one curious passage he admits that a man can be a properly baptized Christian and yet not have received the Holy Spirit. It serves as an illustration in a long argument to show that man was not created perfect from the beginning, not because of any defect in God's power, but because of his own inability to receive perfection all at once. A child cannot receive perfect food from the beginning but only milk. The incarnation of Christ is like that milk with which a mother feeds her child; the gift of the Spirit is the bread of immortality which God sends when we are ready to bear it. When St Paul says to the Corinthans, 'I fed you with milk and not with solid food' (1 Cor 3.4), he meant that, although they had learnt about the incarnation, the Spirit had not yet come to rest on them because of their quarrels and weakness. The apostle had the power to give them the food of the Spirit, 'for whoever the apostles laid hands on received the Spirit', but they were unable to receive because of their weakness (*Adv. Haer.* IV, 38,1-2). It is possible that this passage rests on Irenaeus's own experience that real spiritual break-through and consequent openness to charismatic gifts does not always accompany conversion and baptism, but may be delayed. However this may be, his distinction between re-birth from water and the Holy Spirit, on the one hand, and a being given to drink of the Spirit on the other, may well lie behind the distinction which Cyprian is making with regard to baptism and hand-laying.

From Cyprian we learn that the reception of the Spirit through the laying on of the bishop's hands could sometimes be separated from baptism by a gap of years. This could happen firstly in the case of those baptized during sickness by presbyters and lesser clergy, and secondly in the case of those baptized by heretics who were later received into the Church. This possibility provided occasion for theological formulation as to the effect of the separated rite.

A contemporary of Cyprian, Pope Cornelius, in a letter to Fabian, Bishop of Antioch, says that the schismatic bishop Novatian was baptized during an illness, but had not afterwards 'received the other things which it is necessary to receive according to the rules of the Church', and had not received the consignation of the bishop. 'Since he has not received these things', he says, 'how can he have the Holy Spirit?' (Eusebius, *Hist.* VI, 45,15). It is doubtful whether Fabian would have known of any such 'rule of the Church', but the custom to which Cornelius refers seems to have been known in the African Church. One writer maintains that it is necessary for salvation that such baptisms be supplemented either by the laying on of the bishop's hand or by the special mercy of God (*De Rebapt.* 10), yet he admits that many die without receiving episcopal hand-laying (*ibid.* 6). Cyprian holds that in such cases God will supply all the graces which are necessary and that those baptized in emergency are in no way inferior to other Christians (*Epist.* 69,12ff). He does not make any mention of a necessity for them to receive hand-laying on recovery, though he seems to be familiar with the custom of their doing so (*Epist.* 73,9). Some fifty years later the Spanish council of Elvira decreed that those baptized in emergency by a layman and those baptized in country districts by a deacon when no bishop or priest was present must be 'perfected' by the laying on of the bishop's hand, but should they die before this can take place they will be saved nevertheless (cc. 38,77). The interesting point here is that baptism by a presbyter seems not to need this 'perfecting', whereas in Rome and Africa at this date it was firmly held that only the bishop can confer the Spirit.

The quarrel between Pope Stephen and Cyprian about the rebaptism of heretics brought about some much needed theological reflection. Heresy and schism were a great problem for the Church at the beginning of the third century. The Catholics were convinced that, in spite of all the charismatic gifts in which the schismatic sects seemed to abound, the Holy Spirit was only to be found in the Catholic Church to the exclusion of all heretic bodies. (It is interesting that this position was maintained in the Church until it was formally changed by the Second Vatican Council, Decree on Ecumenism, n. 3). In view of this conviction some churches, both in the East and in the West, considered that the sacraments administered in these heretical and schismatic groups, especially baptism, were without value, and therefore they rebaptized those who had received baptism outside the Church but later desired admission to Catholic communion. Under Cyprian's leadership this practice was adopted by several councils of African bishops. Pope Stephen objected to this innovation and insisted that the traditional practice be followed: converts should not be rebaptized, but hands should be laid on them 'for penitence'.

The importance of this controversy for our purpose lies in the light it throws upon the meaning attached to this hand-laying. All the other documents relating to the contro-

versy, whether they support Cyprian or Stephen, understand the gesture mentioned by the Pope as a laying on of
the hand for the reception of the Holy Spirit. There is not
necessarily any contradiction here. At this epoch it was possible to receive penance only once in the course of a Christian life, and perhaps a second time on one's death-bed. By
grievous sin Christians deprived themselves of the Spirit; so
after the period of penance the bishop's hand was laid on
the penitent so that he might receive the Spirit again.

Pope Stephen declines to take up a theological argument
and took his stand on tradition: 'There must be no innovation.' Yet, if we can believe Cyprian and his supporters, he
maintained that the baptism administered by heretics
brought about the remission of sins with the rebirth and
sanctification of the candidate, but it did not confer the
Holy Spirit, since heretics do not have the Spirit and cannot
confer him. Converts, therefore, needed to receive the Holy
Spirit by the laying on of a Catholic bishop's hand. Against
this Cyprian argues (*Epist.* 73,6, 2; cf. *Epist.* 74,5):

> If a man baptized outside the Church and accord-
> ing to an inadequate faith can receive the remission
> of sins, he can also receive the Holy Spirit according
> to the same faith. There is no necessity, when he en-
> ters the Church, for hands to be laid on him that he
> may receive the Spirit nor for his consignation. Either
> he can receive both outside the Church by his faith,
> or those who are outside receive neither.

Firmilian of Caesarea, who supported Cyprian, uses the
same argument, but since, as seems likely, he would have
used the Antiochene rite of baptism, in which hand-laying
for the reception of the Spirit is not distinct from the baptismal act itself, his argument has more force: either one accepts that this rite produces both the remission of sins and
the gift of the Spirit, or it is totally invalid and must be repeated. In either case any further hand-laying is meaningless (*apud* Cyprian, *Epist.* 75,8,12).

24

Pope Stephen's position was supported by the anonymous African author of the *De Rebaptismate* mentioned above, but his theology is remarkable for its eccentricity. He distinguishes baptism in water from baptism in the Holy Spirit. To the first he assigns a merely preparatory and vaguely consecratory effect; remission of sins and reception of the Holy Spirit are the effects of that 'baptism in the Spirit' which was foretold by the prophets and promised by Christ, which the apostles received at Pentecost and individual Christians receive through the laying on of the bishop's hand. When baptism is celebrated by the bishop this 'baptism in the Spirit' follows immediately upon water-baptism, but it can be separated from it as we have seen. Since the convert has already received water-baptism from the heretics, this must not be repeated; but he still needs to receive the baptism of the Spirit which alone avails to salvation.

The controversy about rebaptism was eventually ended by the adoption of the practice championed by Pope Stephen. In 314 the Council of Arles decreed that those baptized outside the Church, who at their baptism had confessed the Catholic creed, were to be received to communion by the imposition of the bishop's hand and the invocation of the sevenfold Spirit (c. 9(8)). The arguments used on both sides in the dispute make it clear that, in parts of the Western church at least, a distinction was drawn between the effects of baptism and the reception of the Holy Spirit. There was also agreement that the Holy Spirit could be given only by the imposition of the bishop's hand. There seems, however, to have been some confusion as to the meaning of this reception of the Spirit and as to how it differed from the work of the Spirit in baptism.

A century later a little more light begins to be thrown on the meaning of the two rites by bishops from other parts of the Western church. St. Hilary, bishop of Poitiers from c.353 to 367, seems to understand that the Spirit descends upon the Christian only after the washing of baptism. The result of this descent of the Spirit is that he is anointed with heavenly glory and is made a son of God (*In Matt.*, 2,6). He even speaks of baptism and the reception of the Spirit as two sacraments (*In Matt.*, 4,27). St Ambrose, bishop of Milan from 374-397, has left us two works in which he explains the effects of Christian initiation. He describes two distinct operations of the Spirit. In baptism God regenerates the candidates and forgives them all their sins through water and the Holy Spirit. Then after the baptism in the font comes the perfecting 'when at the invocation of the bishop the Holy Spirit is poured out, the spirit of wisdom and understanding, the spirit of counsel and of force, the spirit of knowledge and of piety, the spirit of holy fear, as it were seven powers of the Spirit' (*De Sac.*, III, ii,8). He characterizes this rite of perfecting as a 'spiritual sealing', since in addition to the laying on of the hand it comprised the tracing of a cross on the forehead. Ambrose makes it clear that the reception of the Spirit is conceived in terms of the traditional seven gifts enumerated by Isaiah (11.2ff). We have already seen that the Council of Arles speaks of the reception of the sevenfold Spirit; other texts refer to the reception of the Paraclete Spirit.

Looking backward from the time of St Ambrose it is possible, amidst all the confusion of doctrines, to discern a certain consistency in the doctrine of the Western Fathers. In Hippolytus there is an idea of a filling with the Spirit that comes after the laver of regeneration and is connected with a special grace to serve God according to his will. In Cyprian this is connected with Irenaeus' distinction between regeneration in the Spirit and being given to drink of the same Spirit. Here by means of the doctrine of the seven gifts of the Holy Spirit we have a similar conception of special grace to assist the Christian in the task of living the Christian life. There is no confusion between the work of the Spirit in justification and rebirth, and this other grace of assistance in the business of living: the Spirit is received through the laying on of the hand, not for forgiveness of sins or regeneration, but as the Paraclete, the counsellor and comforter. It is this same aspect on which the later liturgical texts will insist.

Back in Africa a change was taking place in the rite. At the time of Tertullian and Cyprian the rites which followed the immersion had been three: anointing, laying on of the hand and signing with the cross on the forehead. In the writings of St Augustine the last of these seems to have disappeared and the second is merged with the first so that all the emphasis is placed on the anointing. Tertullian had connected the anointing with the immersion rather than with the rite by which the Holy Spirit was given, but Augustine speaks of the anointing as the principal rite for the giving of the Spirit. After his time we hear no more from Africa of the laying on of the hand for the giving of the Spirit.

Augustine speaks of the post-baptismal anointing as the sacrament or sacred sign of the spiritual anointing which is the Holy Spirit himself (*in Joann*. 3,5). Like baptism it holds a very sacred place in the class of outward visible signs (*Petil*. II, 104,239). Its relation to baptism is best illustrated from his sermon to the neophytes. Here he described how through the Lenten fasts and exorcisms they were ground like wheat, in baptism they were mixed with water so that they might take on the form of bread, the body of Christ. But bread needs to be baked in the fire and this fire is supplied by the chrism which is 'the sacrament of the Holy Spirit' who showed himself in tongues of fire. He inspires them with charity by which they burn for God; by this flame they are baked into the bread which is the body of Christ (*Serm*. 227). If baptism makes members of the body of Christ, it is only the special gift of the Holy Spirit which bakes the dough into bread, and this gift is charity. The charismatic gifts to which Irenaeus could point as proof of the Spirit's activity in the Church seems to be unknown to both the Catholics and the Donatists in Africa at that period. 'Who

27

now expects that those on whom hands are laid for the reception of the Spirit will suddenly begin to speak in tongues?' But this is no reason for any to think that they have not received the Spirit. If they find in themselves the love of God and the love of the peace and unity of the whole Church throughout the world, they will know that they have received the Spirit, for as St Paul says: 'God's love has been poured into our hearts through the Holy Spirit who has been given us' (*In 1 Joann.* 6,10; *Bapt.* III, 16,12; *Ser.* 269,1).

It was this text of Romans 5.5 which showed Augustine the solution to the old quarrel about rebaptism, which was still so important to the Donatists. The principal effect of the Holy Spirit was this pouring forth of God's love. Those who have cut themselves off from the Catholic Church manifestly do not possess this gift, for if they did they would cease their schism. It was necessary, therefore, to distinguish between the sacrament of baptism, which could be validly received even by a Simon Magus, the operations of the Spirit such as those listed by St Paul in 1 Corinthians 13, which can take place even in wicked men and which are all nothing without charity, and the invisible working of the Holy Ghost through love, which only the good can possess and which preserves them in the unity of the Catholic Church. The Donatists had true sacraments but their lack of the gift of charity deprived their sacraments of effect. When they were converted to the Catholic Church there was need only to lay hands on them that they might receive this gift of charity which they had lacked and all the sacraments which they had received would take effect. The hand-laying itself could be repeated, unlike baptism, for it was nothing but a prayer made over a man that he might receive the Spirit who pours God's love into the heart (*Bapt.* III, 16,21).

Augustine did not try to attribute the gift of charity exclusively to the hand-laying or anointing which followed baptism, for he well understood that there could be no rebirth, no forgiveness of sins, no conversion without charity. He has recourse to a doctrine very similar to what we have already seen in Irenaeus and Cyprian: 'It is one thing to be born in the Spirit, another to be fed by the Spirit.' The Christian is born in the Spirit through the rebirth of baptism, but the gift which was foretold by the prophets and promised by Christ is the gift of charity poured out in our hearts by the Holy Spirit (*Ser.* 71,12,19). The man who loves God and keeps the commandments already has the Spirit, but having him he merits to have him more fully and having him more fully he loves more. The disciples already had the Spirit when the Lord promised them a Paraclete, for without the Spirit they could not even have called him Lord, but they did not yet possess him in the way the Lord had promised they would possess him (*In Joann.* tr. 74). 'He is invoked, therefore, over the baptized so that God may give them, as the prophet says, the Spirit of wisdom and understanding, the Spirit of counsel and force... the spirit of knowledge and piety... the spirit of the fear of the Lord' (*Serm.* 249).

Later writers were to find here a theology on the basis of which they could work out a distinction between baptism and confirmation; Augustine, however, had no occasion to address himself to this problem directly. He had resolved the questions about rebaptism with a distinction between the sacrament and the grace of the sacrament – a distinction which he applied not only to baptism and orders, but also to the sacrament of anointing (*Petil.* II, 104,230). The questions posed by the practice of following a clinical baptism by later episcopal hand-laying did not arise for him, since in his day the presbyter seems to have performed both hand-laying and anointing (*Serm.* 351,12). In spite of his constant references to the conversion of the Samaritans in Acts 8, he never sees it as proof that the bishops alone have the power to confer the Holy Spirit through the laying on of their hands as other writers do. Indeed he is much opposed to the idea

29

that any man might have the power to give the Spirit (*Trin.* XV, 26,46; *Epist.* 149,15), and he sees the rite of hand-laying as a form of prayer (*Bapt.* III, 16,21).

The writings of Augustine did much to spread the replacement of episcopal hand-laying by chrismation as the principal rite for the conferring of the Holy Spirit, which was already in process before his time. The earliest legislation reserving to the bishop the right to consecrate chrism is of the same period. Already in the time of Cyprian great importance was attached to the consecration of the chrism on the altar during the Eucharist, and this was, no doubt, usually done by the bishop and his clergy together. When it became usual in Africa for the chrismation to be performed by the presbyters as the rite by which the Holy Spirit was given, the episcopal consecration of the chrism took on a new importance; it was the only way in which the link between the reception of the Spirit and communion with the bishop could be manifested in the rite. The bishop laid his hand, as it were, on the chrism which was then applied by the presbyters; thus the prayer and handlaying of the bishop reached the candidates by means of the chrism. This is probably the reason why Councils of Carthage in 390 and 398 insisted that presbyters must not consecrate the chrism themselves. In Spain the same rule was formulated by the first council of Toledo in 398/400.

The same injunction is repeated by Pope Innocent in a letter to Ducentius of Gubbio, but with a different purpose in mind; for in Rome the rite by which the Holy Spirit was conferred remained strictly reserved to the bishop. Rome was probably the first of the churches to have to deal with the problem posed when the number of faithful had become too great to form one liturgical assembly under their bishop. It had developed a system of parish churches throughout the city in which the Sunday Eucharist was celebrated and baptism administered. The visible unity of these churches with the bishop's church was manifested at the Eucharist by placing in the chalice a piece of the bread consecrated by the Pope and sent round to the presbyteral churches. Similarly at the baptismal ceremonies on Easter night the presbyters were wont to anoint the candidates with chrism blessed by the Pope, but this anointing was not considered as the rite by which the Holy Spirit was given. The ancient Roman rite described by Hippolytus contains two anointings after baptism, one performed by the presbyters immediately after the immersion, and another performed by the bishop on the forehead along with the consignation after the laying on of his hand. Pope Innocent, therefore, writes to the Bishop of Gubbio in 416:

> Concerning the consignation of infants, it is clear that this may not be done by any but the bishop. For presbyters, although they are priests of the second rank, do not have the fullness of the pontificate. That this pontifical rite – to perform the consignation or to give the Paraclete Spirit – belongs to the bishops alone is shown not only by the custom of the Church but also by that reading of the Acts of the Apostles which asserts that Peter and John were directed to give the Holy Spirit to those who were already baptized. For it is lawful for the presbyters, whether they baptize in the presence or the absence of the bishop, to anoint the baptized with chrism, but with chrism which has been consecrated by the bishop. They are not allowed to seal (*consignare*) the forehead with the same oil, for this pertains to the bishops alone when they give the Paraclete Spirit (*Epist.* 25).

The rite designated here as consignation or the giving of the Paraclete Spirit seems slightly different from that described by Hippolytus (see comparative tables p. 118ff.). In the earlier rite, after the hand-laying and accompanying prayer there followed an anointing of the head with oil poured from the bishop's hand and after this the forehead was marked with the sign of the cross. Here the anointing and the signing seem to have become one rite of signing the forehead with oil. Our earliest Roman liturgical document must have been composed at least a century after the letter of Pope Innocent but there is no reason to suppose that the rite had undergone much change in the meantime. In the Gelasian Sacramentary we read:

Then when the infant has come up from the font he is signed on the top of the head with chrism by the presbyter with these words:

The Almighty God, Father of our Lord Jesus Christ, who has given new birth from water and the Holy Spirit and has given you remission of all your sins, himself anoints you with the chrism of salvation in Jesus Christ our Lord unto eternal life.

He replies: Amen.

Then the sevenfold Spirit is given them by the bishop. To seal them (ad consignandum) *he lays upon them his hand with these words:*

Almighty God, Father of our Lord Jesus Christ, who have given your servants new birth from water and the Holy Spirit, and granted them the remission of all their sins, do you, O Lord, send into them your Spirit, the Paraclete, and give them the spirit of wisdom and understanding, the spirit of counsel and might, the spirit of knowledge and goodness and fill them with the spirit of the fear of God: in the name of our Lord Jesus Christ, with whom you live and reign, ever God, with the Holy Spirit through all ages of ages. Amen.

Then he signs them on the forehead with chrism saying:

The sign of Christ unto eternal life.
He replies: Amen.
Peace be with you.
He replies: And with your spirit.
Then while a litany is chanted he goes up to his seat and says:
Glory be to God on high.
(*Gelasian Sacramentary,* I, 44).

The first anointing in this rite, like that in Hippolytus and the anointing in Tertullian and Cyprian, belongs to the baptism itself and is not connected with the rite of giving the Holy Spirit. This is sufficiently indicated by the rubrics. At the baptismal ceremonies over which a presbyter presided, this anointing would be followed at once by the Mass and first communion leaving the rites reserved to the bishop to be supplied later. During the fifth and sixth centuries various meanings were ascribed to this anointing by the presbyter after baptism. Pope St Leo (440-461) seems in one passage to see in it the sign that in baptism the candidate comes to share in the royal dignity of Christ and is also anointed priest with him (*Serm.* 4,1). The Roman deacon, John, writing in the early sixth century comments as follows:

He is next arrayed in white vesture and his head anointed with the unction of holy chrism, so that the baptized person may understand that in him a kingdom and a priestly mystery have met. For priests and princes used to be anointed with the oil of chrism, priests that they might offer sacrifice to God, princes that they might rule their people. For a fuller expression of the idea of priesthood, the head of the neophyte is dressed in a linen array, for the priests of that time used always to deck their head with a certain mystic covering. All the neophytes are arrayed in white vesture to symbolize the resurgent church... so that clad in a wedding garment he might approach the table of the heavenly bridegroom as a new man (*Epist. ad Senarium,* 6).

33

Another curious document from the same epoch called the *Liber Pontificalis,* which contains brief notices on the lives and deeds of all the popes, says that Pope Sylvester (314-335) ordered that this anointing with chrism by the presbyter should take place immediately after the immersion 'on account of the danger of death'. Although this notice tells us nothing reliable about the time of St Sylvester, it shows us that in the time of its author it was possible to consider the postbaptismal anointing in Rome as a precautionary measure lest baptized infants should die before they could receive episcopal consignation.

The rite *ad consignandum* given in the Gelasian sacramentary remains with few changes the basis of the present Roman rite of Confirmation. The laying on of hands is performed over all the neophytes together. The prayer given is similar to that in Hippolytus (p. 16 above), but whereas the latter simply asks that the candidates may be filled with the Spirit to receive grace to serve God according to his will, here we have the enumeration of the gifts of the Spirit according to Isaiah. As we have seen, the reception of these seven gifts characterizes the grace of the spiritual signing for St Ambrose (above p. 26) and the grace of the chrismation hand-laying for St Augustine (above p. 27-29). A clear doctrine seems to be emerging. On the one hand there is baptism by water and the Holy Spirit with its positive aspect of rebirth and its negative aspect in the remission of sins, both of which are inconceivable without the activity of the Holy Spirit. On the other hand prayer is made that the candidate may possess the Spirit to the full extent of Christ's promise, that he might be assisted by the Spirit as Paraclete, and receive his sevenfold gift.

The letter of Innocent and the very name *consignatio* seems to indicate that the hand-laying is no longer thought of as characterizing the rite by which the bishop gives the Paraclete Spirit. In Rome too the emphasis is now on the anointing and sealing with the sign of the cross.

Developments in the East

The Eastern churches had finally come to accept Pope Stephen's ruling on the admission of convert heretics during the course of the fourth century. There is a canon of Laodicea, probably not earlier than 380, which decrees that certain listed heretics should be received into the Catholic Church, not by hand-laying but by chrismation with holy oil. Another canon of the same collection orders that the newly baptized should be anointed with heavenly chrism after their baptism. During the last quarter of the fourth century post-baptismal ceremonies for the giving of the Holy Spirit begin to appear in rites of many churches in the East. There is a series of sermons explaining the rites of initiation to the newly baptized which are usually attributed to St Cyril, bishop of Jerusalem from c. 350-386, but which are more probably to be ascribed to his successor John (386-417). Cyril himself writes as if he considered that the Spirit with all his gifts was simply given in baptism (*Cat.* III, 4); in this series of sermons, however, the baptismal immersion is followed by an anointing with scented ointment of the brow, the ears, the nostrils and the breast, which not only takes on all the significance which in the rite of Antioch was attributed to the pre-baptismal anointing, but is clearly a rite which is thought to confer the Holy Spirit. By baptismal immersion the candidate is said to be baptized into Christ, to have put on Christ, and to share the fashion of his glorious body, but they do not have the right to be called Christians until they have received 'the emblem (or antitype) of the Holy Spirit'. Just as when Christ came up from the Jordan the Holy Spirit rested upon him, so the candidates, immediately after their baptism, receive an anointing which symbolizes Christ's anointing with the Spirit to preach glad tidings to the poor. The scented oil of this anointing, once invocation has been made over it, is no longer simple balm but the gift of Christ and the Holy Spirit. Anointing is

35

made on the brow to remove shame and enable the candidate 'to reflect with uncovered face the glory of Christ'. The ears are anointed to give spiritual hearing, the nostrils so that the candidates may know that they are a sweet savour of Christ before God. They are anointed on the breast so that, having put on the breastplate of justice, they may resist the manipulations of the devil; 'for just as Christ, after his baptism and the descent of the Holy Ghost, went to triumph over the devil, you also, after holy baptism and mystic anointing, have put on the armour of the Spirit and can triumph over the enemy' (*Cat. Myst.* 3).

Clearly we have here what we would consider two sacraments and the interpretation of the different effects of the two rites is not altogether different from what we have seen emerging in the West. About the same date there is evidence of the gradual introduction of a post-baptismal anointing with chrism into the rite of Antioch. It has already been shown that the catechetical instructions of Theodore of Mopsuestia, delivered perhaps in 392, are very close to those of John Chrysostom both in rite and in theology. The only difference between them is that, after the baptismal immersion and the clothing with the white garment, Theodore says that the candidate is signed by the bishop on the forehead and perhaps we are to understand that this signing was done with oil. It is accompanied by the formula, 'N. is sealed in the name of the Father and of the Son and of the Holy Spirit'. Theodore is quite explicit that the Holy Spirit is given by the laying on of the bishop's hand as he immerses the candidate in the font. When, therefore, he comes to comment on this sealing all he can say is: 'By this invocation of the Father, the Son and the Holy Spirit you are given the sign and the manifestation that the Spirit has come also upon you, that you have been anointed by him and that you have received him by grace, that you possess him and that he remains in you'. (*Hom. Cat.* 3). Since according to Theodore the Holy Spirit is actually given in the act of immersion, this rite of consignation can be no more for him than a ritual illustration of the fact.

The growing pains of the post-baptismal ceremonies in the rite of Antioch are apparent in the *Apostolic Constitutions* which were compiled about 400. The third book reproduces and enlarges the passage from the *Didascalia* already mentioned (p. 12 above). At the end of this passage the compiler adds: 'And after that let the bishop anoint with chrism those who have been baptized'. He has no explanation of this additional rite because the prebaptismal anointing has already been associated with the sharing in Christ's royal priesthood and spiritual baptism (c. 16). In Book VII the prebaptismal anointing is called 'participation of the Holy Spirit', while the post-baptismal chrismation is merely called the seal of the covenant (c. 22). It would seem therefore that the post-baptismal rite is something new for which the compiler can find little meaning, but later on in this same seventh book he strikes a very different note. The anointing before the immersion is now merely 'the first preparation for baptism' (c. 42). After the baptism the bishop is instructed to anoint the candidate with chrism and recite a prayer to the effect that the sweet odour of Christ may continue upon him and that, now he has died with Christ, he may arise and live with him. Then follows a strange rubric:

> Let him say these and the like things, for this is the efficacy of the laying on of hands on every one; for unless there be such a recital made by a pious priest over every one of these, the candidate for baptism does only descend into the water as do the Jews, and he only puts off the filth of the body, not the filth of the soul (c. 44).

The Pseudo-Denis, who also includes a post-baptismal chrismation in his rite, interprets it by reference to the symbolism of the perfume which bears witness that the initiates have been united to the Spirit (*Hier. Eccles.* III, 8). These post-baptismal rites were still unknown in the liturgy of

Constantinople in the middle of the fifth century and Theodoret, Bishop of Cyrrhus in Syria from 423-458, seems un-
familiar with them. But some form of post-baptismal rite
for the giving of the Spirit was eventually adopted by all the
churches which had radiated from Antioch.

The Eastern churches met the difficulty which was posed
by the general adoption of infant baptism by permitting the
whole rite to be performed by a presbyter and thus preserv-
ing a unified rite of initiation which included baptism, chrismation and first participation in the Eucharist. The Byzantine rite, as we know it from manuscripts dating back to the
eighth century, preserves the prebaptismal anointing almost
as it is described by Chrysostom and Theodore of Mopsuestia; it is an anointing with the oil of gladness. After the baptism the bishop or priest recites a prayer to the effect that
God, who has given new birth to his servants enlightened
by water and the Holy Spirit and has forgiven them all their
sins, may give them also the seal of the gift of the Spirit and
the communion of the Body and Blood of Christ. After this
each candidate is signed with the scented chrism on the
forehead, eyes, nostrils, mouth and ears with the formula:
'The seal of the gift of the Holy Spirit' (see Whitaker, p.
73).

The Armenian baptismal liturgy, of which the earliest
manuscripts are from the ninth century, includes a similar
post-baptismal chrismation. The prayer which precedes it
asks that God, who has granted regeneration by water and
the Holy Spirit, may render the candidate holy by his truth
and replenish him by the grace of the Holy Spirit, that he
may become a temple for the dwelling of God's holy name
and walk in all the paths of righteousness. The chrismation
is made on the forehead, eyes, ears, nostrils, mouth, the
palms of the hands, the heart, backbone and feet (Whitaker,
p. 57).

So far no mention has been made in this study of the
rites of the church of Alexandria. This is because what little

we know of them indicates that they were more similar to the Western than to the Antiochene type. An early source, dating probably from the end of the fourth century, contains a prayer for the blessing of chrism which includes a petition that those who have been renewed by the washing of regeneration may become through the chrism partakers of the Holy Spirit; and the scanty patristic evidence suggests that this was no new idea for the Egyptian church. The present Coptic baptismal ritual dates in its final form from the fourteenth century. The prayer over the chrism, which follows the baptism, asks that God may bestow the Holy Spirit in the pouring out of the chrism. The candidate is then anointed in about thirty different parts of the body. The priest breathes on him and says, 'Receive the Holy Spirit and be a perfect vessel.' He then clothes the candidate and says over him a prayer of the type we are now familiar with: God who commanded that his servants be born through the laver of new birth and has bestowed upon them forgiveness of their sins and the garment of incorruption and the grace of sonship, is asked to send down upon them now the grace of his Holy Spirit the Paraclete.

By the latter half of the sixth century, therefore, probably all the churches of the East – except perhaps the Eastern Syrian Church – were using a chrismation after baptism as a rite for the giving of the Holy Spirit. This rite, however, was never separated from that of baptism and Eastern theologians gave very little attention to the problems of distinguishing the effects of the two rites. John Damascene (c. 657-749) had very little to say about chrismation in his great systematic work *On the Orthodox Faith*. Simeon of Thessalonica (d. 1429), in his work *On the Sacraments*, treats it separately after his chapter on baptism. He says that it is because of this rite that men are called Christians, and that through it they receive the Holy Spirit. It is the seal of the gift of the Holy Spirit, by which the gifts of the Spirit are received. He connects it with the laying on of hands in the Acts of the Apostles.

39

Nicholas Cabasilas (d. 1371), possibly under influence from the West, devoted much thought to the subject and has left a magnificent summary of the tradition which we have found running through Irenaeus, Cyprian, Ambrose, Augustine and the Roman liturgy. He treats separately the three sacraments of initiation: baptism, chrismation and the sacred table. 'We are baptized in order that we may die his death and rise in his resurrection; we are anointed that we may share with him in the anointing of the kingdom of his deification. For baptism is birth; the chrism means for us operation and movement; the bread of life and the cup of blessing is true food and drink. There is no movement or nourishment before birth. Baptism reconciles a man with God; the chrism provides gifts for the one who has just been made worthy; the power of the table makes the initiate share the flesh of the Christ and his blood' (*De Vita in Christo* II, P.G. 150,521). The operation and movement conferred through the chrism are the charisms and gifts of the Holy Spirit; for even now, he says, the gifts of healing, prophecy and tongues of the early Church are bestowed on a few, but to all the gifts of piety, prayer, love, chastity and others are given, if not immediately upon chrismation – for then they are usually infants – certainly in due time unless they are blocked by sin. The Spirit truly distributes his gifts to the initiates, giving to each as he wills, and the Lord has not ceased to work among those with whom he promised to abide. Whenever any of the virtues or charisms are manifest in a Christian, this is because of the sacrament of the divine chrism. (*ibid*. III, *passim*).

This tradition has continued to the present day and forms part of the current teaching of the theological manuals of the Greek Church. The sacrament is defined as 'that instituted rite by which the bodily members of the baptized person are anointed and his incipient spiritual life strengthened and perfected'. The gifts of the Holy Spirit are said to be poured out for sealing and strengthening. 'Baptism, the birth and entrance of the Christian into the spiritual life in Christ, is completed by the bestowal of all the gifts necessary for that life, and by the firm establishment of the steps of the life opened up by baptism, looking forward to the long course of spiritual conflict in the Christian warfare into which it leads him'. (F. Gavin, *Some aspects of contemporary Greek Orthodox Thought,* Milwaukee/London 1925, pp. 316-324.)

CHAPTER 2

EPISCOPAL CONFIRMATION AS A SEPARATE RITE

In the earlier part of this historical survey we have seen that there were two situations which, in some places, led to a rite for the reception of the Holy Spirit being administered apart from the baptismal ceremony: the first arose when baptism had been administered by a presbyter to a person in danger of death, the second when a convert was received who had been baptized outside the Church. Only in Rome, where presbyters presided at solemn baptismal ceremonies in the parishes, was the separate administration of episcopal consignation a regular feature. During the fifth century the growing custom, and indeed the growing sense of obligation, for Christian parents to have their infants baptized led to a great increase in presbyteral baptisms. In the East, in Africa and in Spain this resulted in the presbyters being allowed to confer the Holy Spirit by chrismation. From the South of France, however, we have evidence of a different solution.

It seems that in this region it was customary for the presbyters to travel round the churches in the country districts and baptize the children. When the bishop was next in the vicinity these children would be brought to him for the laying on of hands. The Councils of Riez (439), Orange (441), and Arles (between 449 and 461) refer to this function of the bishop as *confirmare neophytos,* to confirm the neophytes, and they call the rite itself 'confirmation'. We do not know of any earlier use of these terms in this technical sense. At first the rite in question may have consisted of chrismation and an imposition of the hand, but the Council of Orange in 441 determined that the chrismation should be performed at the time of the baptism by the presbyter, and should not be repeated when later the bishop came to confirm the neophytes. Apparently, in this region as in Africa, when the initiation rites were performed in one complete ceremony with the bishop attending there was only one anointing with chrism. Now, therefore, that the ceremony was often split into two parts, there was a question as to where the chrismation should come. Did it belong to the baptism, as Tertullian and Cyprian thought, or was it part of the ceremony by which the Spirit was received? The bishops at Orange decided that it belonged with the baptism and the presbyters were therefore ordered to take the chrism with them when they went out to the villages. It should not be repeated by the bishop when he confirmed by the laying on of his hand. Their reasoning seems to have been that, since the chrism received its virtue from consecration by the bishop, any presbyter could apply it, the presence of the bishop himself was only necessary for the laying on of the hand.

In this region, therefore, we seem to have a situation which is different from any so far studied. Baptism is no longer administered for the most part in the Cathedral church at the festivals of Easter and Pentecost, though, no doubt, these ceremonies still took place. A large number of children are now baptized in their villages by itinerant priests as and when the occasion arises, and they are brought later to the bishop for confirmation.

How general was this custom by the mid-fifth century? This is difficult to answer. In a work written probably in 379 St Jerome witnesses that 'it is the custom of the churches everywhere for bishops to seek out those who are baptized by presbyters and deacons far from the major cities, that he may lay hands on them for the invocation of the Holy Spirit' (*Dial. Orth. et Lucif.* c.9). At that date this may have still been true in Africa, and probably represents the custom of that part of Italy which was especially under the influence of Rome and neighbouring regions, but certainly not the East or Spain. It is interesting that although Jerome admits the custom, he was not prepared, like Pope Innocent, to insist that only the bishops had the power to confer the Spirit. He thinks the custom exists for the honour of the pontificate and the good order and unity of the Church rather than on any intrinsic necessity dependent on apostolic institution.

It seems that in Southern France it was the geographical situation of the church combined with the desire to retain the custom of episcopal hand-laying that created the problem. Along the seventy-five miles of Road from Rome to Gubbio there were no fewer than nine bishoprics. Where dioceses were only some ten miles across it was not difficult to bring children to the bishop for baptism and confirmation. In the provinces of Vienne and Narbonne, where bishoprics like Orange, Arles, Aix and Riez were some fifty miles apart, it was a different matter. Here large distances and the fact that infant baptism was now accepted as the norm for those born of Christian parents combined to produce a rite of episcopal confirmation which was separate from the baptismal ceremonies. It must have been difficult to impress upon the faithful living in remote areas that it was not enough for them to have their infants baptized, but that they must also bring them to be confirmed by the bishop as soon as he came within reasonable distance. What was to be gained by this additional rite which was not given in baptism? It is not surprising, therefore, that from the same region we should have a sermon designed to explain this point. Its author was Faustus, Abbot of the famous monastery of Lerins and then Bishop of Riez, and it was preached on the feast of Pentecost some time between 451 and 470. It chanced that this sermon was to have a very profound effect upon the later theology of confirmation in the West and so it is worth quoting at length.

'In those days, says the Lord, I will pour out my Spirit

upon all flesh.' Such are the riches of the supreme goodness! What the imposition of hands now bestows upon each at the confirmation of the neophytes, the descent of the Holy Spirit at that time conferred upon all the assembly of the faithful.

But because we have just said that the imposition of hands and confirmation can add some strength to him who is already reborn in Christ, some may ask: What good can the ministry of him who confirms do for me after the mystery of baptism? I see, he may say, that we do not receive so much from the font if afterwards we have need of something else in addition.

It is not like this, beloved; listen to me. Military proceedings require that when a commander receives a man into the number of his soldiers, he should not only put his mark upon him, but also equip him with arms suitable for fighting with. So for a baptized man the blessing [of confirmation] is a giving of arms. You have given a soldier; give him also the implements of warfare. What good is it for a parent to bestow great wealth on a small child unless he also provides him with a guardian? The Paraclete is precisely such a protector, counsellor and guardian of those who are reborn in Christ. Therefore the divine word says: 'Unless the Lord guard the city, in vain do the watchmen keep vigil.'

So the Holy Spirit, who descended upon the baptismal waters bearing salvation, gave at the font all that is needed for innocence: at confirmation he gives an increase for grace, for in this world those who survive through the different stages of life, must walk among dangers and invisible enemies. In baptism we are born again to life, after baptism we are confirmed for battle.

In baptism we are washed, after baptism we are strengthened. Thus for those who die at once the benefits of rebirth are sufficient, but for those who survive the aids of confirmation are also necessary. The rebirth of itself saves those who are soon to be received into the peace of the blessed age, confirmation arms and equips those who are reserved for the conflicts and battles of this world. He who after baptism comes to death immaculate in the innocence he has acquired is confirmed by death itself – for after death he is no longer able to sin.

Now if we should want to ask what the apostles were to gain after the death and resurrection of the Lord from the advent of the Holy Spirit, it is the Lord himself who clearly explains it. 'The things I say to you you cannot bear now. When the Spirit of truth comes he will teach you all truth.' You see that: *when the Spirit of truth is poured out upon us, the faithful heart is enlarged for prudence and constancy*. Therefore, before the descent of the Holy Spirit the apostles were terrified to the point of denial: after his coming, despising deliverance, they are armed even for martyrdom. In this way by Christ we are redeemed; by the Holy Spirit we are illumined with the gift of spiritual wisdom, we are built up, we are instructed, we are equipped, we are perfected so that we can hear those words of the Holy Spirit: 'I will give you understanding and I will equip you for the way in which you are to walk.'

* From the Holy Spirit we receive the gift of being made spiritual, for 'the unspiritual man does not receive the things which are of the Spirit of God.' From the Holy Spirit we receive the ability wisely to discern between good and evil, to love what is just and reject

what is unjust, to fight against malice and pride, to resist impurity, divers enticements and defiling unworthy desires. From the Holy Spirit we receive the gift of being set on fire with the love of life and the glow of glory, that we may be able to lift our minds from earthly things to the divine things on high.* To this end we have received rational faculties, the gifts of nature and the reparation of second birth...

In this remarkable homily Faustus provides a very clear answer to the question which the separation of the two rites had given rise to: What does this second rite of confirmation add to one who has been baptized? It is not simply a question of the gift of the Spirit, for the Spirit is already active in baptism – he descends upon the baptismal water bringing salvation; in the font he gives all that is needed for innocence. Nor is the gift of baptism incomplete in its kind. But there exists a gift of a different nature conferred by the Holy Spirit: this is the assistance which is so essential for the struggle of the Christian life. The one is like an act of creation, the other an aid to living. The one is the gift of infancy in Christ, the other is strength for the warfare of the adult Christian life. The distinction between new birth from water and the Holy Spirit, and the assistance of the Spirit for the subsequent growth, goes back to Irenaeus and beyond and is probably the basis on which the Western distinction of the two rites has always rested. The application to this distinction of the military analogy and the idea of the Christian warfare is quite natural, although for John Chrysostom this was a result of the undifferentiated initiation rite. Confirmation is seen very much as the sacrament of the reception of the Holy Spirit for growth and the whole struggle of Christian living. There is little new in all this language except, perhaps, the neat distinction and distribution of effects between the two rites, but when we read the sermon against what we know of its author we can see how it expresses the very personal convictions of his monastic life at Lerins. He had learnt that it was one thing to receive God's free gift in baptism, but another to live out the Christian life in conformity with the new nature received. It was the human effort needed in the struggle against the wisdom of this world, which made the difference between ultimate salvation and damnation, and for this human effort the Christian needed to be armed with the prudence and constancy which are the gift of the Holy Spirit. Confirmation is thus characterized as the sacrament of the spiritual life.

The events of the period which followed hard upon the delivery of this sermon, however, were not favourable to the development of confirmation as an independent rite. The inroads of pagan barbarians into the region and the consequent disruption of the ecclesiastical organization made the regular episcopal visitation of the countryside impracticable. All the evidence which has come down to us about the rites of initiation practised in Gaul and Northern Italy during the following two and a half centuries indicates that the separate episcopal rite which had been called confirmation was quite unknown. In the liturgical books from these regions we find simplified rites of Christian initiation which could be carried out in entirety by a simple priest. They include baptism, chrismation, and communion and were clearly not thought to be lacking in any way for want of episcopal intervention. The full gift of the Spirit was thought to be conferred through the chrismation with chrism consecrated by the bishop.

Our next group of Roman documents on the subject are almost two hundred years later than the letter of Pope Innocent mentioned above (p. 31). In 603 Gregory the Great reminds the bishops of Sicily that his predecessor had ordered that the presbyters were not to be put to undue inconvenience when the bishops were travelling round for the consignation of infants (*Epist.* 13,18; Ewald p. 388). But conditions in Sicily were more difficult than those in central Italy. He has to advise one bishop, who was sick, that he should visit only those churches which are easily accessible, so that those who have been baptized shall not remain without consignation (*Epist.* 10,45; Ewald p. 262). One of his letters on this subject was later to cause theologians much trouble. To Januarius, Bishop of Cagliari in Sardinia, he writes objecting to the practice of presbyters sealing the infants on the forehead, and this consignation being then repeated by the bishop. He says that the presbyters should anoint only on the breast. This ruling, however, upset many and Gregory wrote again:

> It has reached us that some were scandalized because we forbade the presbyters to touch with chrism those who are to be baptized. We acted according to the ancient use of our church; but if any are made completely sad by this thing, we concede that, where bishops are wanting, presbyters ought to touch with chrism the baptismal candidates even on the forehead. (*Epist.* 4,26; Ewald p. 261).

It seems likely that Sardinia had begun to copy the Greek custom by which chrismation for the reception of the Spirit was performed by the presbyters when no bishop was present. Gregory allows this to continue. He did not, therefore, regard the ancient rule of the church of Rome to be of absolute importance.

Confirmation in Spain at the time of St Isidore

Towards the end of the pontificate of Pope Gregory, in the year 600 Isidore became Archbishop of Seville. The Roman province of Spain had been over-run by several barbarian hordes and was now the territory of the Visigoths, except for Cartagena and some land along the coast which had been reconquered by the Emperor Justinian. The Visigothic king had turned from Arianism to Catholicism in 587, and although many of his Arian bishops had followed his exam-

49

ple, the Arian Church was still a power. The Spain that Isidore knew, therefore, was a land of many peoples and faiths, and this must be borne in mind when considering what he has to say on Confirmation. Isidore was widely read in the Fathers and cognisant of the customs of many different parts of the church. Through his brother Leander's friendship with Gregory he was familiar with the customs of Rome but also with those of Byzantium, where Gregory and Leander had met, especially as the Byzantine customs were used in Greek speaking Cartagena. There was a Syrian settlement in Seville, and he may also have known the Coptic rites, for Coptic silver begins to appear in the peninsula by 600. Isidore wrote for posterity and his works had great influence, but they are not always a good guide to the liturgical practice of the Spain he knew.

Spanish dioceses were much larger than those of Italy and we have already seen evidence from the Romano-Hispanic church that an anointing with chrism by the presbyter was considered sufficient to perfect initiation and confer the Holy Spirit. Isidore takes this tradition seriously, for he places chrismation along with baptism and the Eucharist in his famous definition of sacraments, saying: 'They are called sacraments because under the clothing of corporal things the divine power secretly brings about the salvation which is the effect of these same sacraments' (*Etimol*. VI, xix,40). The same trio are mentioned as sacraments by the Fourth Council of Toledo (633), over which Isidore presided. Sometimes Isidore will quote Tertullian and speak as if the effect of baptism was entirely negative and that of the chrism positive: 'For as in baptism the remission of sins is given, so through the anointing sanctification by the Spirit is achieved' (*ibid*. 50). He follows the traditional interpretation of the rite of anointing, that it makes the baptized share in the priestly and kingly dignity of Christ, the anointed one. He is also familiar with the rite of the laying on of the bishop's hand for the gift of the Spirit, and he mentions this

50

in his description of baptism after he has dealt with the meaning of the chrismation.

> But after baptism the Holy Spirit is given by the bishops with the laying on of hands. This is what took place in the Acts of the Apostles... [he quotes Acts 19.1-7 and 8.14-18, and continues] We can only receive the Holy Spirit, we cannot give it, but we invoke the Lord that he might be given (*De Offic.* II, 27; cf. Augustine, *De Trin.* XV, 26,46).

He then quotes the letter of Innocent given above (p. 31). Isidore's aim in this work is to be encyclopedic and to bring together the opinions of past authorities on many matters. As to the actual practice, everything we know of the time leads to the conclusion that episcopal hand-laying was not practised, except perhaps when baptism was done in the presence of a bishop. It is true that in the second Council of Seville, called by Isidore, a list of rites which are the privilege of bishops is drawn up and among them mention is made of 'to give the Holy Spirit by the imposition of the hand upon the baptized faithful', 'to sign the forehead of the baptized with chrism'. This was only a small local council. In the great Fourth Council of Toledo which Isidore organized, where sixty-six bishops resolved ambitiously to abolish all diversity in the carrying out of the Church's sacraments and offices and in which many liturgical laws were passed, no mention is made of episcopal hand-laying nor are presbyters forbidden to give the Holy Spirit through chrismation. Isidore must have seen that it would be impossible to impose uniformity in this matter even had he wanted to.

Confirmation in England

The situation in Gregory's new English mission contrasts greatly with that of Isidore's Spain. England was virgin territory apart from the Celtic church to the North and West.

St Augustine was free to implant what liturgical customs he thought best, and despite Pope Gregory's advice to pick and choose whatever was of worth or beauty in the churches he had passed through, it seems that he settled for the Roman rite he was familiar with. In England, then, from the beginning of the mission, episcopal confirmation was deemed a necessary part of Christian initiation. The large crowds which St Augustine is said to have baptized – as many as ten thousand on one day – must presumably have received the full rite of initiation according to the Roman custom, and the same is true of the different royal baptisms described by Bede. The bishops did as much as they could; St Paulinus is said to have spent thirty-six days baptizing a whole tribe in Glendale; but inevitably much of the preaching and baptizing had to be left to presbyters, who according to the Roman tradition could not give a complete initiation. It was necessary, therefore, for the bishops to travel round to complete this initiation by the laying on of the hand. Bede reports that St Cuthbert toured the rural parts so that he might preach 'and lay his hand on those recently baptized so that they might receive the Holy Spirit'. In the Penitential of Theodore of Canterbury we find the statement: 'A bishop may confirm in a field if it is necessary.' There were very few bishops in England to cover the vast areas and we can only conclude that many must have gone without confirmation. The Roman tradition of episcopal consignation had grown up in the very different circumstances of urban Rome and the tiny dioceses surrounding it. The English clergy, however, did not look upon episcopal confirmation merely as a Roman tradition: they simply held that presbyters had no power to confer the Spirit. Commenting on the eighth chapter of Acts, Bede (d. 735) writes:

Note that Philip, who evangelized Samaria, was one of the seven. If he had been an apostle he would himself have been able to lay on his hand that they might receive the Holy Spirit, [and he quotes the letter of

52

Innocent I, see p. 31] 'This pertains to the bishops alone... for it is lawful for the presbyters, whether they baptize in the presence or the absence of the bishop, to anoint the baptized with chrism, but with chrism which has been consecrated by the bishop. They are not allowed to seal the forehead with the same oil, for this pertains to the bishops alone when they give the Paraclete Spirit' (*In Act.* VIII).

In his commentary on St Luke he remarks that after the Last Supper Christ led those who had fed on his Body and Blood up to the Mount of Olives to teach 'that all who are baptized into his death were to be confirmed with the highest chrism of the Holy Spirit' (*In Luc.* VI, 22). But in his commentary on Mark he repeats the doctrine of the two receptions of the Holy Spirit.

But the Holy Spirit rested upon him not only from the time when he was baptized by John in the Jordan, but rather from the time when he was conceived in the Virgin's womb. The Spirit was seen to descend at the baptism as a sign that spiritual grace would be conferred on us in baptism, and that, born in the remission of sins by water and the Spirit, a further grace of the same Spirit would be given from heaven through the imposition of the hand (I, I).

Confirmation in the Carolingian Epoch

It seems likely that it was the English missionaries who reintroduced episcopal confirmation into the Germanic and Frankish kingdoms. St Boniface attached great importance to confirmation in his reform of the Continental churches. In his first German Council of 742/3 and the Council of Soissons in 744, it is ordered that 'whenever according to canonical law the bishop goes round his parish to confirm the people, the presbyters should always be ready to receive the bishop and help with the collection of the people who are to be confirmed there'. If such confirmation tours had been unknown in the Frankish territories for more than two hundred and fifty years, the tone of the canon is surprising. All the evidence, however, indicates that there was great resistance to the custom of episcopal confirmation throughout the next century.

Charlemagne came to power in 754 and showed great interest in the reform of the Church throughout his realm which had been begun by Carloman and Pepin. Fidelity to Roman liturgical customs was held to be an important part of this reform. Charlemagne wanted his realms to have a uniform liturgy like that which prevailed in the Byzantine empire. Liturgical books were sought from Rome and detailed descriptions of papal ceremonies called Roman *Ordines* were made and adapted to Frankish needs. This liturgical reform affected the rites of Christian initiation principally in two ways: there was an attempt to return to the ancient Roman practice of celebrating it only at Easter and Pentecost and thus to stop the administration of baptism here and there as the need arose, and there was a new insistence upon the importance of episcopal confirmation.

The administration of the Christian rites of initiation at Easter and Pentecost seems always to have been regarded as the ideal in Gaul, but the importance placed upon infant baptism acted against its observance. In 585 the Council of Macon complains:

> We learn from our brethren that Christian people, not observing the appointed day for baptism, baptize their children on other days and on the festivals of martyrs, so that at the holy Pasch only two or three can be found to be regenerated by water and the Holy Ghost. And therefore it is our decision that none shall henceforth be permitted to do such things except they are compelled by serious illness or approaching death to have their children baptized. And therefore we re-

quire all men, being recalled by this present admonition from their errors or ignorance, to observe the first Sunday of Lent with their children, and having received the imposition of hands on certain days, and being anointed with the holy oil, they may rejoice in the festivities of the appointed day and be regenerated by holy baptism (canon 3).

The motivation behind such legislation was not just liturgical conservatism. There were no Sunday schools or catechism classes at this period, and any instruction which children would receive would come from their parents or sponsors. It was therefore important that the Church should be satisfied that the parents knew the Lord's prayer, the creed and the rudiments of the faith. The ceremonies of the catechumenate during Lent enabled some control to be kept on the situation. Such rulings, however, proved ineffectual — no doubt to the great harm of the Church. In 769 Charlemagne again made it a law. In 802 the Frankish church officially accepted the authority of the Roman collection of decretals which included the rulings of Popes Siricius and Leo I restricting baptism to the vigils of Easter and Pentecost, but the fact that this legislation had to be constantly reiterated by provincial councils during the ninth century shows that it was not easy to change the habit of centuries.

The second point in which the liturgical reform affected the rites of initiation was in the renewed insistence on episcopal confirmation. Again in 769 there was legislation to enforce the episcopal visitation of the diocese for the administration of this rite. The ceremony was to be found in the liturgical books of Roman provenance which were now in circulation. In the year 784 Charlemagne insisted that the Roman liturgical practices should be followed throughout his domains. A sacramentary for use in the papal liturgy of the day, which is now known as the *Gregorian Sacramentary*, was sent to him by Pope Hadrian. It was furnished with a supplement by adapting it to the needs of the Frankish Church by Alcuin, the king's English advisor, and many copies were made of it at the Royal scriptorium. The sacramentary contained the ancient Roman prayer for the laying on of the bishop's hand after baptism. The Supplement contains the rite for the administration of solemn baptism at Easter and Pentecost. Here, after the clothing of the candidate in the white garment, appears the following instruction:

If the bishop is present, it is fitting that he be at once confirmed with chrism and afterwards communicated. And if the bishop is not present let him be communicated by the presbyter (H. A. Wilson, *The Gregorian Sacramentary*, p. 163).

Alcuin evidently does not expect the bishop to be present, for he gives neither description of the rite nor the prayer to be said. The ceremonies are described in the other Roman books in circulation and can be reconstructed as follows.

While the priests were busy administering baptism and the anointing which followed it, the bishop seats himself in his chair in the church. The children in their white garments are brought before him. According to some books he then gives to each a stole, a chasuble, a chrismal cloth, and ten coins (*Ordo XI* and .he *Sacramentary of Gellone*). They are arranged in a circle and he says the confirmation prayer 'with his hand raised over the heads of all' (*Sacramentary of St Eloy*), 'confirming them with the invocation of the sevenfold grace of the Holy Spirit' (*Ordo XI*). The Prayer contained in the *Gregorian Sacramentary* is still used in the present Roman rite of confirmation (*cp.* p. 32).

Almighty and everlasting God, who hast given new life through water and the Holy Ghost to these thy servants, and granted them forgiveness of all their sins, send down upon them from heaven thy sevenfold Holy Spirit, the Paraclete, the spirit of wisdom and of understanding, the spirit of counsel and of fortitude, the spirit of knowledge and of piety, fill them with the spirit of the fear of thyself and in thy goodness sign them with the sign of the cross of Christ. Through the same Jesus Christ, thy Son, our Lord, who lives and reigns with thee for ever and ever.

After the prayer the bishop makes the sign of the cross on each of them with his thumb dipped in chrism, saying either: 'The sign of Christ unto eternal life' (*Regin. 313* and *Gellone*), or, 'In the name of the Father and of the Son and of the Holy Spirit' (*Ordo XI*). He then gives to each the kiss of peace saying: 'Peace be with you.'

Frequently there follows in the manuscripts a rubric like this one from the *Sacramentary of Gellone*: 'Take care that this is done for all and let them not neglect this, for then they confirm everyone who is baptized with the name of Christianity.' The necessity of the rite is made even clearer by the *Roman Ordo XV*:

> The baptized children, if they have the bishop present, ought to be confirmed with chrism; which, if they are not able to obtain the bishop on the day itself, they should do without delay, as quickly as they can obtain him (Andrieu, III p. 120).

When the ruling on the two times for baptism was observed, more children would be baptized in the cathedral church in the presence of the bishop, but the baptismal ceremonies were also carried out in all the other towns and larger villages of the diocese on the same days. Even Alcuin does not suppose that confirmation will often be administered immediately after baptism. Clearly it is no longer considered as part of the baptismal ceremony. In some cathedrals, even at the Easter vigil, it was placed after the communion, and Alcuin himself recommends the Sunday after Easter as a very fitting time for those baptized at the vigil in the cathedral to receive confirmation (*Epist.* 143 Ed. Duemmler; MGH, Epp VII, p. 202f.).

For two and a half centuries previously, Christian initiation in Gaul had consisted of one single ceremony which could be carried out, if necessary, by a simple priest. It comprised baptism, anointing with chrism for the reception of the Holy Spirit and first communion. The partisans of the reform maintained that this was not sufficient and that another ceremony must be added either after communion or a week later, or as soon as possible. Naturally opposition was aroused. What authority had they for saying that the form of initiation in the Gallican books was not sufficient and what was the meaning of this additional rite which would put the faithful to such inconvenience?

In answer to the first of these questions those in favour of the reform pointed not only to the Roman liturgical books, but to the rulings of the popes, especially Innocent's letter to Decentius of Gubbio. The works of Isidore of Seville were also used as proof that the Roman rule was the norm of orthodoxy. As to the value and meaning of the rite, Alcuin was content to reply that while in baptism the Christian is endowed by grace for eternal life, through the laying on of the bishop's hand 'he receives the Spirit of sevenfold grace so that he may be strengthened by the Holy Spirit to preach to others' (*Epist.* 134). The question was taken up at greater length by Alcuin's pupil Rabanus Maurus. He is at pains to reconcile the reintroduced rite of episcopal confirmation with the theology of Christian initiation generally accepted which was based upon the presbyteral rite of the Gallican books. It is therefore necessary for him, as for St Isidore before him, to accord proper importance to the post-baptismal anointing performed by the priest as a rite by which the Holy Spirit is conferred. Quoting from Isidore he enumerates baptism and chrism and the body and blood of the Lord as sacraments and lists the virtues of the anointing, again drawing on Isidore.

> For after the baptized has come up from the font immediately he is signed on the head by the presbyter with holy chrism, prayer being made at the same time that he may be a partaker of the kingdom of Christ, and from Christ can be called a Christian. It is writ-

ten also in the Gospel thus: 'And when Jesus was baptized he went up immediately from the water, and be-
hold the heavens were opened and he saw the spirit
descending like a dove and alighting on him.' It is
well therefore that in baptism the anointing with
chrism should follow, because the Holy Spirit, who
through the chrism sanctifies believers with the ad-
mixture of his power, at Jesus' baptism immediately
descended upon him in the form of a dove. The dove,
which at the time of the flood carried an olive-branch
green with leaves back to the ark, was the fore-
shadowing of this, signifying that the Holy Spirit,
through the anointing in baptism confers on the faithful the green life of heavenly grace (*De Cler. Inst.* I,
28).

Rabanus has no wish to argue that the Holy Spirit was not
given in the Gallican rite of initiation; he clearly admits that
the anointing confers the Spirit. Why then episcopal confirmation? He wants us to put this question in a different way: it
is not the ancient rite of episcopal hand-laying which should
be questioned, but rather the custom of presbyteral anointing.
Having recourse to the *Liber Pontificalis* (see above p. 34) he
explains that this latter rite only came into existence as a
cautionary measure, lest children should die before they
could be confirmed. Confirmation, therefore, is the true
sacrament of the Holy Spirit: the presbyteral anointing only
an anticipation of it. He therefore continues:

It is written in the Apostle: 'You, brethren are not in
the flesh but in the Spirit, if the Spirit of God lives in
you. If any one does not have the Spirit of Christ he
does not belong to him.' It is clear that whoever is not
of Christ cannot be partaker of his kingdom. So it is
necessary that he who has been baptized should immediately be succoured by the anointing with chrism,
so that receiving participation in the Holy Spirit, he
may not appear alien from Christ.

Having conceded full value to the presbyteral anointing he then turns to the episcopal confirmation.

> Finally the Holy Ghost, the Paraclete, is conferred upon him by the chief priest through the laying on of the hand, that he may be fortified by the Holy Spirit to preach to others the gift which he himself gained in baptism, when he was endowed by grace with eternal life. For the baptized is signed by the priest on the top of the head, by the bishop on his forehead. The first anointing signifies the descent of the Holy Spirit upon him to consecrate a dwelling for God; by the second it is declared that the sevenfold grace of the same Holy Spirit has come upon the man with all the fullness of sanctity for the knowledge of the truth. On the former occasion, the Holy Ghost himself, when the bodies and souls are cleansed and blessed, willingly descends from the Father to sanctify his own vessel by his visitation. On this latter occasion he comes into the man with this intent, that the seal of faith, which he has received on his brow, may make him replete with heavenly gifts, and strengthened by his grace to bear the name of Christ fearlessly before the kings and rulers of this world and preach it with a free voice (*op. cit.* I, 30).

So the grace of confirmation is boldness in confessing Christ. It is possible that Alcuin and Rabanus arrived at this conclusion through a reading of the sermon of Faustus, but if so they have narrowed Faustus' perspective considerably and taken his military simile too seriously. Did they have in mind primarily the large number of adult converts baptized after Charlemagne's conquests to the East? It is certainly more difficult to apply this doctrine to infants confirmed as soon as possible after their baptism. One contemporary bishop, Magnus of Sens, who was very unlikely to baptize any adults, prefers to say that the rite of confirmation confers a strengthening in the true faith by the Holy Spirit.

Rabanus has one more interesting argument which we will need to refer to again. There is nothing strange, he says, in the fact that we need to be anointed twice with the same chrism to receive the same Holy Spirit.

> For the same Holy Spirit was given to the apostles themselves twice over – once, that is, upon earth when after his resurrection the Lord breathed upon them, and once from heaven, when after the ascension of the Lord he came upon the apostles on the day of Pentecost in fiery tongues, and granted them the ability to speak in the tongues of all the nations (*ibid.* I, 30).

The victory of the Carolingian reformers was to be consolidated in a strange way. Much had been done to restore liturgical observance, Church structures, and the study of theology, but the power of the king and the nobles to interfere in ecclesiastical affairs had grown and been confirmed by law. The very life of the Frankish church depended on its being able to escape from this secularization. The lay aristocracy, who benefited greatly from their ability to choose bishops and help themselves to the money of abbeys and bishoprics, were not impressed by the protests of the bishops nor by the laws passed in their synods. The only authority which could command their respect was that of the ancient decretals of the Roman Pontiffs. Unfortunately there was nothing sufficiently clear in the canonical collections. In an age in which it was not unusual for ancient texts to become interpolated or to be adapted to present needs, the temptation to forge what the written tradition did not contain was great. When at the royal assembly of Epernay in 847 the reform programme of the bishops was once more turned down by the nobles, the patience of the clergy was at an end and certain leading ecclesiastics decided to embark on an ambitious piece of forgery. By 852 the great work known as the canonical collection of Isidorus Mercator was in circulation. The compilers mined the libraries of Europe for ancient texts which could be adapted to their purpose, and they produced an impressive collection of decretals attributed to early popes which contained in abundance the legislation so badly needed in relation to the surbordination of bishops to their metropolitans, and the supreme authority of the pope not only over all the bishops but over the rulers as well. Obviously if the collection had contained nothing except texts to support the reform programme of the Frankish bishops it would have been suspect. The really important decrees had to be inserted casually here and there among matters relating to many points of ecclesiastical discipline, and to provide this other material the compilers took the opportunity to furnish some clear expressions of doctrines which had the stamp of orthodoxy but on which few clear texts existed. In this way they were able to cover most of the points which had been in dispute in early days of the reform a generation or so previously, and among these confirmation figured largely.

Their bold enterprise was all too successful. Within a few years it was accepted and was cited even by Pope Nicholas I, who probably knew it was a forgery. By the canonists and theologians of later generations the authenticity of the work was accepted without question. Many of its decrees were incorporated into later collections and finally enshrined in the Decretals of Gratian whence they continued to influence theology until the present century.

The subject of episcopal confirmation is mentioned in no less than five separate decretals and from this insistence we can only conclude that in the middle of the ninth century not only did many neglect to receive it, but that opposition to it must still have been expressed. In a decree attributed to St Clement, the third Bishop of Rome, reference to confirmation by a bishop and its necessity is inserted into a passage of a third-century work dealing with the necessity of baptism (Hinschius, p. 63). A spurious letter of Gregory I classes confirmation with baptism and the consecration of churches as rites which may only be repeated where there is genuine doubt that they have been already performed (*ibid.* p. 749). The *Decretum Eusebii* was to achieve a greater importance and must be quoted.

> The sacrament of the imposition of hands is to be held in great veneration. It may not be performed except by the high priests. At the time of the apostles we do not read or know of its being performed by any but themselves, and it may never be administered or carried out except by those who now hold their office. If any should presume otherwise, it should be held as unlawful and void, nor should it be thought to have any place among the Church's sacraments (*ibid.* p. 242).

Two other decretals cite the sermon of Faustus of Riez thus assuring for this work a renown and an authority which it would not otherwise have gained. The first of these, attributed to Pope Urban (222-230), borrows from Faustus to explain the law which it desires to instil.

> All the faithful must receive the Holy Spirit after baptism by the imposition of the bishop's hand, so that they may become full Christians, because 'when the Holy Spirit...' etc. (as above, p. 46, the passages between asterisks. *Hinschius* p. 146).

The second, attributed to Pope Melchiades or Meltiades (310-314), was to provide the mediaeval theologians with the whole first half of the sermon (up to the second asterisk on p. 46 above) prefaced with the following authoritative ruling:

> Regarding your enquiry as to whether the imposition of the bishop's hand is a greater sacrament than baptism, know that both are great sacraments. And since one is given by a minister of greater dignity, that is by the high pontiffs, it must be held in greater veneration. But these two sacraments are so closely conjoined that they may only be separated by premature death, and the one cannot be rightly administered without the other. For the one may save without the

other if death intervenes, the other cannot. Therefore
it is written: 'In those days, says the Lord, I will pour
out my Spirit on all flesh.' 'Such are the riches of the
supreme goodness' etc. (Hinschius, pp. 245-246).

By means of these decretals the compilers brought about a
turning point in the theology of episcopal confirmation. In
the first place, what previously had been recognised as a
custom of the Roman church and was attested by the letters
of Innocent and Gregory is now clearly stated to be necessary for all except when death intervenes; without it a man
cannot be a full Christian. Secondly, they have canonized
Faustus' interpretation of the rite, although, because they
do not quote the second part of his sermon, they place the
emphasis on Christian adulthood and the 'warfare of
Christ', on what Rabanus had called 'strength for the fight',
rather than on the whole work of the Holy Spirit in the
Christian life.

During the tenth century the liturgical books compiled by
the Franks which contained the various pontifical rites were
brought to Rome and began to be used there, for culture in
that city had reached a very low ebb. It was in this way that
the ceremony of confirmation, which the Franks had received from Rome, returned to that city slightly ⸺⸺shed
and the theological understanding worked out by the Carolingians went with it. The tenth-century rite differed very little from that described on p. 32f., except that the words
which the bishop says as he signs the neophyte with chrism
have become a closer parallel to the baptismal formula. The
Romano-Germanic *Pontifical of Mayence,* composed about
950 and brought to Rome early in the following century
gives two formulas:

I confirm you in the name of the Father and of the
Son, and of the Holy Ghost (CVII, 40; Vogel II, p.
163);
and
I confirm you and sign you in the name of the Father,

and of the Son, and of the Holy Ghost (XCIX, 387).

By the twelfth century *Pontifical of the Roman Curia* this formula has further evolved to become:

N. I sign you with the sign of the cross and I confirm you with the chrism of salvation in the name of the Father, and of the Son, and of the Holy Ghost (XXXII, 33; Andrieu p. 239).

From this time on we begin to find the rite of confirmation written out separately, apart from the rite of baptism at Easter, so as to be more convenient for the bishop. This rite differs very little from that of the *Roman Pontifical* of 1596 which is still in use. There is, however, one difference which attracted a lot of attention. The kiss of peace which the bishop gave to each of the candidates (see p. 33) has now become a slap on the cheek! This is due to a thirteenth-century canonist called Durandus of Mende who made a new edition of the Pontifical. It must have been difficult to give the kiss of peace to infants and we can suppose that the kiss degenerated into a caress. Durandus made this into a blow to show that the candidate had received the grace of 'strength for the fight'.

Confirmation in Scholastic Theology

The labours of the Carolingian epoch provided the scholastic theologians with their source material, and to a large extent, especially in the matter of confirmation, they determined the questions to be debated. The scholastic sense of history was not well developed: they accepted the documents collected by the canonists at their face value. Their genius consisted rather in their penetrating understanding of the tradition which had reached them and their development of a systematic theology. The investigation of the notion of sacrament which until this time had been applied to a large range of rites and prayers, signs and events, was one of their earliest achievements (see *The Theology of the Sacraments*). By the time of Peter Lombard (c.1100-1160) the definition of a sacrament had been so refined as to make possible the isolation of what we now call the seven sacraments. Lombard defines a sacrament as 'a sign of God's grace and a form of invisible grace but in such a way as both to bear the image of that grace and be its cause' (*Liber Sententiarum* IV, distinction I, c.4). The seven sacraments which he distinguishes have the common property of being causes of the grace they signify. He also distinguishes in each sacrament what he calls the substance, i.e. a material element or action, from certain words which he calls the form of the sacrament. All the other ceremonies connected with the sacrament exist merely for its beauty and solemnity and are not of necessity. Thus the anointing with chrism by the priest, to which Isidore and Rabanus attached such importance and which in Gaul and Spain had been considered as the rite by which the Holy Spirit was bestowed, is now seen as having no proper sacramental value; it merely gives solemnity to the sacrament of baptism and signifies some aspect of its mystery, without causing what it signifies.

In his short section on confirmation Lombard produces a patchwork of quotations from the False Decretals, Rabanus and Gregory I relating to the following subjects:

a) The Form of the sacrament.

b) It may only be administered by a bishop.

c) Its effect is the gift of the Holy Spirit for strength.

d) The relation of confirmation to baptism.

e) That it cannot be repeated.

His work was used as the standard theological textbook in all the mediaeval universities and the great developments of scholastic theology were worked out in commenting on his text or discussing the problems it raised. The most convenient manner to set out the scholastic teaching on confirmation, therefore, will be to arrange it under the headings of Lombard's treatment.

a) *The Substance of the Sacrament and its Institution*

For the bishops at the Council of Orange in 441 the laying on of the bishop's hand was quite distinct from the anointing. The Carolingians not only saw the two acts as one but accorded most importance to the bishop's anointing with chrism. Thus when the scholastics were asking what the matter and form of confirmation might be, it did not even occur to them that they might be the ancient prayer: 'Almighty and everlasting God, who hast given new life through water and the Holy Ghost' etc. (see p. 56f. above), and the imposition of the bishop's hand over the group which accompanies it, though these are clearly the most ancient elements of the Roman rite. They were looking for a material element which could in some way be a sign of the grace received and a form of words which would make the significance of the material element clear. Even in the ordination rite they preferred to see the handing over of the chalice etc. as the matter of the sacrament rather than the laying on of hands. They were also conditioned by a long tradition connecting the gift of the Holy Spirit with an anointing. And so they declared the matter of this sacrament to be the chrism, or more precisely the signing of the forehead with chrism which was combined with a laying on of the hand; the form they held to be words spoken by the bishop during this gesture, even though these tended to vary from book to book.

The question of the institution of confirmation was much more difficult. William of Auxerre (before 1231) taught that it was instituted on the day of Pentecost, but this was not satisfactory as no indication of matter and form was given. Some held that it had been instituted by the apostles, but they had conferred the Spirit by the laying on of hands. St Albert (1249) held that Christ had truly instituted the sacrament, and if he chose to confer the Holy Spirit by breathing on his disciples, this was because as author of grace he could confer it how he wished. The apostles themselves, he declared, had never administered the sacrament without using the form found in the Roman Pontifical. To justify this statement he made an interesting distinction between two types of confirmation. One is for the general good of the recipient and could be done by any holy man of meritorious life. This the apostles frequently used, imparting the Holy Spirit by prayer and the laying on of their hands. But the sacrament of confirmation in which the Spirit is given for strengthening was never used by the apostles except with the proper form. The proof of this, he says, can be seen in the writings of Denis the Areopagite, who knew the apostles. Unfortunately Albert did not know that the works attributed to Denis were written in the fifth century.

A succession of Franciscan masters including Alexander of Hales and William of Melitona held that the sacrament had been instituted by the Church. St Bonaventure (1250-1252) argues that Christ neither instituted nor celebrated the sacrament of confirmation, because the Spirit was not given in fullness till after the Ascension. The apostles, therefore, were confirmed by the Holy Spirit without intermediary or sacrament. They in their turn confirmed others without using any words or any element, because when they gave the Spirit miraculous signs appeared which sufficed to indicate the grace received. It was not till after the death of the apostles that the rulers of the Church, by the prompting of the Holy Spirit, instituted the matter and form of this sacrament to which the Spirit himself gave power. Another Franciscan, who completed the Summa of Alexander of Hales, even asserts that this was done at the Council of Maux in 845, though the reason for his saying so completely eludes us.

St Thomas Aquinas dismisses this notion as very stupid. To him it is obvious that only Christ could institute the sacraments, and if confirmation were a sacrament it must have been instituted by Christ. He says, therefore, that Christ instituted this sacrament not by demonstrating it but by promising it when he said: 'If I do not go away the Holy

Spirit will not come to you.' With regard to the matter of the sacrament he argues that it was indicated to the apostles in the tongues of flame – since oil is fuel for fire – and in the gift of tongues – for the balsam communicates to others by its scent as tongues by sound. When the miracle of tongues accompanied the laying on of the apostles' hands no sacrament was needed, because the miraculous events were sufficient indication of the grace received, but when these visible signs did not occur the apostles frequently used chrism, as Denis the Areopagite affirms. On these occasions they used the form of words which Christ had commanded them to use, which like many other things are not mentioned in scripture but handed down in the tradition, as St Paul indicated concerning the Eucharist when he says, 'The rest I will settle when I come' (*Summa Theologica*, III, 72, art. 1-4., written about 1272). This was the opinion which found most general acceptance, and St Bonaventure in a later work, the *Breviloquium* (Part VI, c.4), feels obliged to admit that Christ was the initiator of the sacrament and had 'insinuated' it to the apostles.

b) *The Minister of Confirmation*

The Carolingian theologians and the False Decretals left no room for a real debate about the minister of confirmation. Peter Lombard cites on this point the false decretal of Eusebius (see above p. 63) where it is expressly affirmed that the sacrament will be invalid if conferred by any save the bishops, who are the successors of the apostles. Lombard, however, also quotes Gregory's letter to Januarius (see above p. 49), and the import of this letter was hotly debated. How could Pope Gregory grant permission to simple priests to administer confirmation, for no one has the power to dispense from what belongs to the substance of the sacraments? This objection was answered in two ways. St Albert, for instance, argues that he did not intend to grant priests the power to confirm. Either he simply refrained from correcting their ignorant abuse to avoid scandal, or he was permitting them the use of a sacramental, just as blessed bread is sometimes distributed to those who cannot communicate. Others, including St Thomas, argue that the pope has a fullness of power by which he may permit those in lower orders to perform functions which pertain to those of higher rank, just as he can allow priests to confer minor orders. Gregory used this power to avoid a scandal. These ingenious solutions are quite out of keeping both with the ecclesiastical institutions of the time of Gregory and with the liberal policy of the saint in liturgical matters which is apparent from his other letters. The objections which draw proof from Gregory's letter that it is not impossible for a priest to confirm remain unanswered.

c) The Effect of the Sacrament

The Carolingian theologians had made it sufficiently clear what they thought the effects of confirmation to be, and they had given their views so much authority that it was virtually impossible for the scholastics to come to any other view. Peter Lombard points to three effects:

1) A strengthening by the Holy Spirit so as to be able to preach to others what is received in baptism. This is taken from Rabanus.

2) The reception of the Holy Spirit so as to become a full Christian – this is supported by citation of the false decretal of Urban (see above p. 63).

3) Reception of the sevenfold grace with all the fullness of holiness and virtue – this again is from Rabanus.

The Scholastics laboured to make sense of these statements within the framework of their systematic theology. In the first place it was not easy to see why strengthening for the spiritual conflict with internal or external enemies might not just as well be ascribed to other sacraments, especially as the psalm says: 'Bread will strengthen (*confirmet*) the heart of man.' How was the effect of confirmation different from that of the Eucharist? The objection is dealt with by all the scholastics from Alexander of Hales onwards and in answering it they were led deeper and deeper into an analysis of the grace conferred by the sacraments. Some said that confirmation strengthened the intellect and the Eucharist the emotions. Alexander of Hales and Hugh of St Cher (1229-30) said rather that the Eucharist strengthens the Christian's love, while confirmation gave him strength to resist evil. Gueric of St Quentin (c.1242) said that the Eucharist strengthened for the interior life and interior confession of faith, but confirmation was concerned with exterior acts of confession. In this he was later followed by St Thomas.

d) *The relation of confirmation to baptism*

In what sense could it be said that confirmation added something not received in baptism, or that it made the neophyte a perfect Christian? Alexander of Hales followed Faustus in saying that baptism gave a fullness of being, confirmation a fullness of strength. This was no more satisfactory than his saying that baptism conformed a man to Christ, sealing him with his character, while confirmation made him a soldier of Christ. Some made reference to the three anointings of David. Baptism is likened to the first anointing in his father's house while he was still far from having power. Confirmation is likened to his second anointing in Hebron, because by confirmation we are made worthy to reign. The third anointing of David symbolized the anointing of the Christian in glory.

The scholastics came to realize that sanctifying grace, by

which God makes the sinner acceptable to himself, is inseparable both from the moral and theological virtues and from the seven gifts of the Holy Spirit. Thus every baptized person not only has the virtue of faith but also the gift of fortitude. How then could one speak of confirmation as strength for conflict? The answer was to speak of a grace called sacramental grace distinct from sanctifying grace. The latter is conferred by all the sacraments but the former differs according to each. The special sacramental grace of confirmation was strengthening for the struggles of the Christian life, that of baptism was the remission of sin. But all the sacraments conferred or increased sanctifying grace.

It is not possible here to discuss the important but constantly shifting role which the concept of character played in the sacramental theology of the different scholastic schools. All were agreed, however, that confirmation conferred a character because it is one of the sacraments which could not be repeated. St Thomas uses this notion to distinguish the effects of baptism and confirmation. He conceives character as a special deputation, a marking out, or an assigning to the performance of certain sacred actions in the Church. In baptism the character received deputed the Christian to partake in Christ's priesthood both by the worship of the Christian life and by its sacramental expression. In confirmation he is deputed to those actions which belong to the spiritual fight against the exterior enemies of the faith. In baptism he receives power to do whatever pertains to his own salvation, since this is the sacrament of rebirth into the spiritual life: in confirmation he receives the power to proclaim the faith before others, for confirmation is the sacrament of Christian adulthood and it belongs to the adult to communicate socially. The apostles, he says, before they received the fullness of the Spirit at Pentecost remained in the upper room persevering in prayer, but after Pentecost they were not ashamed to speak publicly of the faith even before enemies (*Summa Theologica*, III, 72,5). In this way

St Thomas integrates the ideas of Faustus into his own scheme of sacramental theology.

Much of the work done by the scholastics on the theology of the sacraments was canonized at the Council of Florence in 1439. The doctrine on the sacraments set forth in the Decree for the Armenians is largely taken from St Thomas's opuscule *De Articulis Fidei et Ecclesiae Sacramentis*. This document marks the official acceptance of the doctrine of the seven sacraments, three of which imprint a character. The paragraph on confirmation follows St Thomas's text closely except for enlarging on the necessity for the minister to be a bishop.

> The second sacrament is confirmation, of which the matter is chrism, made from oil and balsam signifying the aroma of good reputation and which is blessed by the bishop. The form is: 'I sign you with the sign of the cross and confirm you with the chrism of salvation in the name of the Father and of the Son and of the Holy Spirit.' The ordinary minister is the bishop, and while a simple priest is competent to perform other anointings, this must not be performed except by a bishop. For only of the apostles, whose representatives the bishops are, do we read that they gave the Holy Spirit by the imposition of the hand. This is made clear in the Acts of the Apostles (and they cite 8:14-17). Confirmation is given in the Church in place of that imposition of the hand. There is record, however, that occasionally simple priests, by delegation of the Apostolic See for a reasonable and urgent cause, have administered this sacrament of confirmation with chrism blessed by the bishop.
>
> The effect of this sacrament is that the Holy Spirit is given in it for strengthening as it was given to the apostles on the day of Pentecost, so that the Christian may boldly confess the name of Christ. For this reason the one to be confirmed is anointed on the brow,

which is the seat of shame, and lest he should blush
to confess the name of Christ and especially his cross,
which, as the Apostle says, is a scandal to the Jews
and stupidity to the gentiles, he is marked with the
sign of the cross (Dz 1317).

The Council of Trent had nothing to add to this. It merely
insisted that as one of the sacraments of the New Law confirmation must have been instituted by Christ, and that the
ordinary minister of the sacrament is the bishop.

The Suitable Age for Confirmation

For the Carolingian reformers the rite of confirmation was,
in principle, to be administered as soon as possible after
baptism, but in fact a period of several years must often
have elapsed before there was an opportunity for receiving
it. Not only were parents slow to appreciate the importance
ascribed to the rite by the canonists, but the bishops themselves were often negligent in making their rounds. Some of
the evidence suggests that the reception of confirmation often depended upon the chance of encountering a bishop on
the road. The Old *Penitential of Theodore* says that confirmation could take place in a field if necessary, and the bio-
grapher of St Hugh of Lincoln (d. 1200) sees it as a sign of
exceptional virtue that this prelate was wont to dismount
from his horse to confer the sacrament.

In 1240 a synod at Worcester and one at Chichester in
the following year ordered that confirmation take place
within a year of baptism, but about 1280 a synod of Dur-
ham recommends the age of seven years and a synod of Ex-
eter (1287) recommends the age of three. The question of
the most suitable age was discussed by at least one of the
scholastics. In spite of the obvious objection that it was not
suitable to confer on infants a sacrament which gave
strength for confessing the name of Christ before the ene-

74

mies of the faith, William of Melitona (c.1255) came to the conclusion that the time of innocence was the most suitable, since the sacrament would not have any the less effect when the candidate became an adult, but if neglected there was a danger that the infant who died without it might forgo some of the glory he would otherwise have had and the parents would be to blame.

A council held at Cologne in 1280 declared that persons under the age of seven were too young to be confirmed, and the evidence suggests that this opinion was widely held in the fourteenth century. In 1536 another council at Cologne actually uses for the first time the argument which is used so frequently today: 'Before a child has reached the seventh year of his life he will understand little or nothing of what is done, much less remember it.' After this many local councils prohibited the confirmation of children under seven and the *Catechism of the Council of Trent* says: 'Here it is to be observed that, after baptism, the sacrament of confirmation may indeed be administered to all; but that until children have attained the age of reason its administration is inexpedient. If not, therefore, to be postponed to the age of twelve, it is most proper to defer this sacrament at least to that of seven years.' Further than this Rome was never prepared to go. Indeed, all through the sixteenth century it was still not unknown for a bishop to confirm immediately after he had baptized. It is attested in the case of the English royal children, Arthur, son of Henry VII, and the future Elizabeth I. The edition of the *Sarum Ritual* printed for the use of Catholic priests at Douai in 1604 still retains the old rubric: 'If a bishop is present, he could be confirmed at once, and afterwards he should be communicated if of suitable age.' When there was no bishop, the parents were instructed to have the child confirmed when he came within seven miles.

In more modern times Pope Pius XII granted a general permission to parish priests to confirm those in danger of death. This had to be seen in the context of a long series of permissions granted to those not in episcopal orders, especially where the uniate Eastern churches are concerned. It is significant that the rigid mediaeval position on this point should have been so far relaxed, and shows what profound and unintended results an isolated document such as Gregory's letter to Januarius can have in the canonical system of the Western church. The Pope's opening words show how constant the Western theology of confirmation has remained over the last 1100 years, and provide a good point at which to bring this brief historical survey to an end.

> Catholic dogma proclaims that the gifts of the Holy Spirit are conferred in the sacrament of confirmation. Hence the Church is solicitous that children, washed in the waters of baptism, should be refreshed by such a sacrament, by which they obtain the charismata of the Paraclete from above and add strength to the faith received in baptism, so that, anointed with the fullness of grace and signed with the character of a soldier of Christ, they may be recognised and go forth equipped for every good work (*Acta Apost. Sed.* 1946, p. 349).

The new Order of Confirmation which was promulgated together with the Apostolic Constitution *Divinum Consortium Naturae* on 22 August 1971 constitutes the most important statement on confirmation ever made by the Magisterium. In 1963 the Second Vatican Council ordered the rite of confirmation to be revised so that the connection of this sacrament with the whole of Christian initiation be made clearer. It was recommended that a renewal of baptismal vows should precede it and that where convenient it should be integrated into the mass (*Liturgy Const.* n. 71).

Following these instructions the new rite takes the important step of ruling that adult catechumens and children who are baptized at an age when they are capable of receiving instruction should normally receive the three sacraments of baptism, confirmation and communion in one ceremony,

76

even when the bishop cannot be present. The chief aim of this and all the recent liturgical reform has been to make the words and gestures used in the rites express more clearly the holy things which they signify, so that as far as possible they may be found easy to understand and take part in. As there has been a great lack of clarity among theologians concerning the effect of Confirmation, one of the chief aims of the Apostolic Constitution was to provide a clear doctrinal statement.

In the New Testament, the Constitution says, we learn how the Spirit descended upon Christ, at his baptism, to enable him to carry out his messianic ministry. He promised his disciples that he would send the Spirit of truth, who would remain with them for ever and assist them to bear witness to him (Jn 15.26; 14.16; Acts 1.8). On the day of Pentecost the Holy Spirit came upon the disciples in a remarkable manner, making them announce the wonderful works of God, and Peter recognised in this the gift of the messianic age. 'From that time,' the document continues, 'fulfilling the will of Christ, the apostles by the imposition of their hands bestowed on neophytes the gift of the Spirit, which completes the grace of baptism (Acts 8.15-17; 19.5f.). Thus it came about that in the Epistle to the Hebrews teaching about baptism and the imposition of hands is counted among the first elements of Christian instruction. The Catholic tradition rightly recognises this imposition of hands as the beginning of the sacrament of confirmation, which in some way perpetuates the Pentecostal grace in the Church.'

In baptism the neophytes receive the remission of sins, the adoption of the sons of God, and the character of Christ by which they become members of the Church and first share in the priesthood of her saviour (1 Peter 2.5.9.). Through the sacrament of confirmation those who are reborn in baptism receive the ineffable gift which is the Holy Spirit himself, by

77

which they are endowed with special strength and, marked with the character of this same sacrament, are bound more perfectly to the Church and are more closely obliged both to spread and defend the faith by word and deed, as true witnesses of Christ. Confirmation also belongs with the sacred Eucharist, for by partaking of the Eucharist, those who are sealed by sacred baptism and confirmation are inserted in the body of Christ.

It is admitted that many different rites have been used in the bestowal of this gift. The rite of chrismation, however, has long been practised in the East and now features in the majority of the Oriental rites. In the West popes and doctors have maintained that the anointing of the forehead with chrism accompanied by the imposition of hands is alone required for valid confirmation. Since, therefore, this chrismation is a fitting symbol of that anointing with the Holy Spirit which the faithful receive, it has been decided to preserve it. On the other hand the words which accompany this anointing in the Roman rite have varied a great deal up to the thirteenth century. It has seemed preferable, therefore, to adopt the ancient formula of the Byzantine rite which has been in use since the fourth century: *sphragis doreas Pneumatos Hagiou*, 'the seal of the gift of the Holy Spirit'. This formula combines two important scriptural terms. The first is the *dorea Pneumatos Hagiou*. The ancient meaning of the word *dorea* was endowment, donation, dowry, and in the New Testament it is reserved for the gifts of God. In Acts the term is used to specify the outpouring of the Spirit which is the fulfilment of the ancient prophecies (Acts 2.38; 10.45; cf. 8.20). The term *sphragis* designates the seal of the Spirit, a notion already mentioned many times and to which we will return. The Pope continues:

Since, therefore, the revision of the rite of confirmation rightly touches the very essence of the sacrament, by our supreme apostolic authority we determine and establish that what follows shall be observed in the Latin church. The sacrament of confirmation is conferred by an anointing on the forehead with chrism, which is made with an imposition of the hand and by the words: 'Receive the seal of the gift of the Holy Spirit.'

Although the imposition of hands over the candidates, which along with the prescribed prayer precedes the chrismation does not pertain to the essence of the sacramental rite, it is nevertheless to be greatly esteemed as an element which gives integral perfection to this rite and a fuller understanding of the sacrament. It is clear that this imposition of hands differs from the imposition of the hand which follows it, by which the anointing with chrism is made.

The new rite underlines the connection between confirmation and the other sacraments of Christian initiation, by the inclusion of scripture readings, in the homily which follows, in the renewal of the baptismal promises, by the bidding prayers and by the blessing at the end. A translation of the rite will be found in the appendix.

Another significant change concerns the minister of confirmation. The old Roman rule is relaxed to the extent that the bishop is now held to be only the 'originating minister' of this sacrament. It should usually be administered by the bishop himself, but the right to confirm is given not only to other prelates who have territorial responsibility, but also to priests authorised to baptize adult catechumens or children of an age to receive instruction, or those who receive a validly baptized adult into full communion with the church. In danger of death, not only parish priests but also their curates or, in the absence of these, any priest may now confirm. When a large number are to receive the sacrament, the bishop, or whoever takes his place, may be assisted in the administration of the sacrament by priests who hold special office in the diocese, by the parish priests of those to be confirmed and the priests who have been responsible for the instruction of the candidates.

No new ruling is made as to the age at which those baptized in infancy should receive the sacrament. In accordance with the custom of the Western church this is generally to be deferred until the age of about seven years, but permission is given to each episcopal conference to decide that it may be deferred to a more mature age.

CHAPTER 3

THE THEOLOGY OF CONFIRMATION

1. The Gift of the Spirit in the New Testament

Before the Holy Spirit became a theme of doctrine, it was a fact in the experience of the Christian community. Nevertheless the New Testament writers differ greatly in the way in which they treat of this experience. Not only do they assign different places to it in their various theologies of salvation: they also use very different concepts and models to interpret it (in what follows the author acknowledges his especial indebtedness to the article *Pneuma* by E. Schweizer in the *Theological Dictionary of the New Testament*).

One such model was furnished by the writings of the Old Testament. There 'spirit of God' is the name given to God's active power, that is the personal activity of God's will, impinging on Israel as the power of history, achieving a moral and religious object. This idea of the power of God as spirit, is closely allied to the idea that God spoke and the world came into being at his word, for the spirit is nothing other than 'the breath of his mouth'. In this sense the Spirit of God is active power which proceeds from God and gives life to the physical world. It has nothing at all to do with the notion of a divine power or substance immanent in nature as the soul of all things. It comes from without and although it is operative in nature may not be identified with it. 'Flesh' or the condition of created weakness is totally other than 'spirit', the power of the divine will. The spirit of God is not only active in history, working out God's inscrutable purposes: it may also fall upon individuals – Othniel, Gideon, Jephtha, Saul, David and the prophets – where it is manifested as the unpredictable and irresistible working of God's power, for those who until then had been comparatively unnoticed, and now come forward as leaders. In such cases ecstatic activity and prophetic speech reveal the working of God's spirit, but the when, the why and the how long of such activity remains inscrutable.

In the Gospels of Matthew and Mark the Holy Spirit is conceived and portrayed almost entirely in these terms as God's power to perform special acts. It is the power which drives Jesus into the desert (Mk 1.12), the power by which Jesus expels demons (Mk 3.28; Mt 12.32), the power which inspires the sacred writers of the Old Testament (Mt 22.43; Mk 12.36). The conception of Jesus is attributed to the Holy Ghost by Matthew in order to affirm that his coming is of the mysterious saving power of God. At the baptism, Jesus is endowed with the same Spirit as were the prophets of old, but he becomes in a unique way the bearer of this Spirit. Henceforth it will be active, not just as mediating God's word, but he will speak in the disciples at the time of their persecution (Mk 13.11). Mark alone mentions a general endowment with the Holy Spirit (1.8), and he must have seen this saying as realized in the outpouring of the Spirit on the community.

For Matthew and Mark as for Old Testament Judaism as a whole, the Spirit is not necessary to salvation but is a power for additional deeds; it does not constitute salvation, but is a sign of the real thing which is still to come. In Joel, for example, the outpouring of the Spirit is a prelude to the catastrophy of the end of time (2.23-33). Salvation is not to be discerned in the mere presence of all kinds of miraculous powers; these are a welcome but basically unnecessary sign of what is to come. Such a notion presented problems for the Greek world where the thought-patterns did not permit the idea of history with its succeeding ages. Thus not only was the delay of the expected *parousia* an embarrassment for the preachers of the Gospel: the very idea of an entirely new age was one which the Greek world had great difficulty in understanding. These difficulties gave rise to a new model for the interpretation of the promise of the Spirit.

In the Hellenistic culture all power was understood as substance. Where for the Old Testament the Spirit was the power of God, the Greeks were inclined to understand Spirit as part of the heavenly world, the divine substance. The coming of the Spirit therefore was for them the heavenly substance breaking into the world. If Jesus was the bringer of the Spirit, then he was the bearer of heavenly substance with which he endowed believers and united them with the heavenly world. The postponement of the *parousia* was not important. The point of the mission of Jesus was to bring heavenly substance, spirit, into the world. Attachment to Jesus was thus attachment to this substance of power, i.e. to the heavenly sphere. Thus it is salvation itself. Combined with the already existing religious systems of the Hellenistic world this idea was to form the basis of Gnosticism.

Paul, the apostle of the Gentiles, was able to take over this thought-pattern and, by purifying it of false ideas, to make it an instrument for the preaching of the Gospel. More than any who preceded him he saw the cross and resurrection of Christ, not as a prelude to the *parousia*, but as the great turning point which inaugurated the new age, the event which brought salvation. The presence of the Spirit was the result of the descent and ascent of the Redeemer, but because this event inaugurates the new age, the new creation in the risen body of Christ, he was able to adopt the Hellenistic notion and depict the presence of the Spirit as that which involves the community in the heavenly sphere, imparting a new heavenly existence.

In Romans 1.3 it is shown that Jesus is the son of David according to his carnal existence and son of God in his spiritual existence; he was 'descended from David according to the flesh, and designated Son of God in power according to the Spirit of holiness by his resurrection from the dead'. Again according to 1 Cor 15.45, Christ becomes lifegiving spirit in the resurrection and is thus able to endow the believer with a 'spiritual body'. Of Adam, who enclosed the whole of humanity within himself it is said, 'The first man Adam became a living being': but the last Adam, Christ, 'became life-giving Spirit'. The exalted Christ is in the sphere of 'spirit'. Turning to him entails entry into this sphere. 'He who is united to the Lord becomes one spirit with him' (1 Cor 6.17). Paul's argument is that the resurrection sets Christ in the sphere of the Spirit and that union with him ensures the believer of a spiritual life which is life in the community, the body of Christ.

Paul is much concerned to correct Hellenistic spirituality through the biblical notion that all is God's gift and God's working. There is no notion that the spirit is something which man naturally possesses and which simply outlasts death. All depends on the creative power of God in Christ. Between the earthly body and the spiritual body there lies a miracle. God, who has raised Jesus from the dead, is already at work in believers by the Spirit, and will also continue to work after their death. The natural man is a sinner who has fallen victim to death, but the one who is righteous in virtue of the work of the Spirit will rise again (cf. Rom 8.11).

Baptism, for Paul, is the moment when the believer enters into the death and resurrection of Christ and thus takes on the new form of 'spiritual' or heavenly existence (Rom 6.3-11). Baptism in the name of the Lord Jesus is also baptism 'in the Spirit of our God' (1 Cor 6.11). The name of the Lord justifies objectively, the Spirit subjectively: 'For in one Spirit we were all baptized into one body – Jews or Greeks, slaves or free – and all were made to drink of the one Spirit' (1 Cor 12.13). Being in the Spirit is the same as being in Christ. It is the foundation of all the Spirit's gifts. Hence one who is in Christ is 'made to drink of the Spirit'.

The activity of the Spirit is seen as the sign and the guarantee of what is to come. Now that Jesus is raised from the dead, the resurrection at the end of time is no longer a vague hope. The activity of the Spirit is the first fruits of

84

the still expected resurrection (Rom 8.22). Along with the idea of 'guarantee' and 'first fruits' Paul uses the image of anointing with the Spirit, reminiscent of the anointing of Jesus, and that of the 'seal': 'But it is God who confirms us with you in Christ, and anointed us, and has put his seal upon us and given us his Spirit in our hearts as a guarantee' (2 Cor 1. 21-22). By all these images he is underlining the one thing: through baptism the Christian is involved in the new creation and the activity of the Spirit as an earnest of future resurrection.

Yet although the Spirit has for him so central a role in salvation, he is yet able to view the Spirit as giver of extraordinary and miraculous feats. The possession of the Spirit can be demonstrated. Among the activities of the Spirit he counts speaking with tongues, the gift of healing and other miraculous powers. That he can presuppose the existence of such powers in Thessalonica and Galatia, in Rome – where he did not found the church – as much as in Corinth shows that this is more than the mere survival of a primitive tradition. He is constantly pointing to such phenomena as the guarantee of what is to come. Yet unlike some other writers in the New Testament, he holds that the manifestation of the Spirit need not necessarily have an extraordinary character. His depreciation of tongues in 1 Cor 12 shows that he thinks that extraordinariness is basically irrelevant as a criterion; it would do just as well as a criterion for the religious experiences of the pagans (1 Cor 12.2). The criteria are rather confession of the Lord Jesus, the building up of the community, and expediency. Thus he brings us to a completely new understanding of the Spirit.

First and foremost the Spirit is the power of faith, the power which mediates supernatural knowledge and determines both the content and the form of the preaching: 'We impart a secret hidden wisdom of God' (1 Cor 2.7). But although, in this passage, Paul uses mystical language to express the content of the message, 'the depth of God', what he is speaking about is God's saving work at the cross, it is simply 'Christ crucified' (1 Cor 1.23; 2.2; 2.8). The whole basis, then, of the transplanting of the believer out of this age into the new creation is the knowledge which the Spirit gives of the crucified Lord. The supernatural quality of this knowledge no longer rests on the fact it is taught ecstatically; the miracle is that man may believe that God has worked for his salvation in Jesus Christ. This supernatural knowledge is not a disclosure of the mysteries of the heavenly world, but the divine act of love manifested on the cross. The Spirit, therefore, is called the Spirit of faith (2 Cor 4.13), and to possess the guarantee of the Spirit is 'to walk by faith' (2 Cor 5.5,7). Not that the Spirit is just a mysterious force which appears prior to faith and explains its origin. On the contrary he finds the work of the Spirit more evident in continued and outgoing belief. The Christian is not only baptized in the Spirit, he is given to drink of the Spirit, nourished by the Spirit 'from faith to faith' (Rom 1.17). Along with faith the Spirit also gives the ability to love as the chief of his gifts and his love is no merely human activity, it is the love of God: 'God's love has been poured into our hearts through the Holy Spirit who has been given to us' (Rom 5.5). The Spirit also enables the believer to pray (Rom 8.15,26). In fact the most characteristic activities of the Spirit are not of the ecstatic or miraculous order. They can be listed as 'love, joy, peace, patience, kindness, goodness, faithfulness, gentleness, self-control' (Gal 5.22-23).

Once the Spirit comes to be regarded as a divine power which is not characterized by the extraordinariness of its operation, but rather in making men believers and enabling them to live as such, then this power can no longer be regarded as a force into whose hands man is helplessly delivered up. Paul ascribes control of the Spirit to the believer (1 Cor 14.32), and exhorts him to be zealous in the Spirit and not to forbid or hamper such activities as speaking with tongues (1 Cor 14.1,39). The Spirit does not rule out rational deliberation (1 Cor 7.40). It is therefore a rational power from God which gives to man – who remains quite distinct from God – the ability to live by it, consciously and deliberately to allow himself to be guided and ruled by it. This is well summed up in the apparently tautologous saying in Galatians 5.25: 'If we are made alive by the Spirit, let us also walk by the Spirit.' Not only is the new life of the Christian sustained by the Spirit at a supernatural level: the Christian is summoned to acknowledge this consciously and to let his whole life be shaped thereby.

The Gospel of Luke and the Acts of the Apostles, written about the year 80, contain a theology of the Spirit which is very different from that of Paul. There is no evidence in Luke's thought of the basic Hellenistic model according to which the Spirit is understood as a kind of divine substance and a breaking in of the divine sphere. Luke seems content with the Judaic model, but he has to modify it to the situation of the time in which he was writing, a time in which the delay of the expected *parousia* had produced a certain malaise in the Christian hope. Luke endeavours to shift man's concentration from expectation of the definitive establishment of Christ's kingdom and concentrate them on the present age, an age of missionary activity by which the end is to be prepared. In this age salvation is assured in two ways, through the continued presence of Christ and through the gift of the Holy Spirit.

Luke does not see Jesus as present to his Church *through* the Spirit, for the Spirit is not seen as mediating the presence of the divine as in Paul. This is evident both from the Gospel and from the Acts. Whereas in Matthew and Mark one has the impression that the working of the Spirit is sporadic in Jesus, for Luke it continues to work in him. The statements about his endowment with the Spirit both at his birth and at the baptism serve two purposes: they distinguish him as one who stands in especially close relationship to God with a unique commission, but they also describe him as a man who receives the Holy Spirit like other men as a gift. He is 'full of the Holy Spirit' (Lk 4.1). At his exaltation he then pours out the Spirit as a gift on the Church (Acts 2.33). Thus the creative power which was active in the birth of Jesus also creates new life in the community, releasing at Pentecost the ecstatic powers of prophecy. It is this 'power from on high' (Lk 24.49) which is to be the chief instrument of the missionary work which will transform the world.

Salvation itself, however, is not the direct work of the Holy Spirit; it is the prerogative of Christ. Nor is salvation for Luke synonymous with the sending of, or the possession of the Holy Spirit. In the Gospel the miracles of Jesus are never ascribed to the Spirit; healing power is associated with the name of Jesus, with faith in Jesus, with Jesus himself. Similarly in the Acts, Jesus remains present to the community in virtue of 'his name'. The apostles heal and preach in the name of Jesus and those who call upon that name will be saved (Acts 2.21). The Spirit does not produce faith; even when Luke wants to emphasize that believing is a miraculous God-granted event, he never attributes it to the Spirit (Acts 16.14; 3.16). Nor does the Spirit forgive sins. Repentance and baptism in the name of Jesus for the forgiveness of sins come first; then only is the Spirit received (2.38). Prayer is not regarded as an act of the Spirit, rather it is the preparation for the receiving of the Spirit. Finally the ideal state of the community can be described without mention of the Spirit (2.42-47).

In many ways Luke's understanding of the Spirit and his function is similar to that of later Judaism. The Spirit is for him above all the Spirit of prophecy. In Lk 12.10 the Spirit against whom it is unpardonable to blaspheme is no longer the power of God manifested in exorcism (cf. Mt 12.25-37; Mk 3.23-29), but the power of God manifested in the inspired utterance of Jesus. Luke presents the phenomenon of Pentecost as though it were chiefly a kind of prophecy, for he emphasizes the fact that all were able to hear the praises of God in their own languages. He also adds the words 'and they shall all prophesy' to the passage of Joel which otherwise he leaves unaltered (Acts 2.18). He sees the new community, therefore, as a community of prophets. Elsewhere the activities most typical of the Spirit are ecstatic speaking in tongues (Acts 2.4; 10.46; 19.6), the sudden inspiration which makes possible the vision of things to come (Lk 1.41,67, Acts 11.28), the ability of the disciples to discern thoughts which are hidden from the natural man and to proclaim to this man what is in his inmost heart (Acts 13.9), insight into the will of God which is otherwise concealed, especially when it gives direction for concrete action (Acts 8.29; 10.19; 11.12; 13.24; 16.6f.; 20.22), but most of all the preaching of the disciples. Only secondarily do we find formulae in which the Spirit is understood as dwelling continually in the individual or in the community. Luke is still attracted to the line of thought which measures the work of the Spirit by its peculiarity. His interest, however, is not in the peculiarity as such; it is in the fact that God gives his community visible signs of his presence and clear directions. He is strongly interested in the visibility of these signs, especially in the Spirit-given preaching which he considers the primary activity of the Spirit in the community.

The new element in the gift of the Spirit to the Christian community does not lie in the Spirit's activity, which remains very much what was expected of the Spirit in late Judaism; it lies in the universality of the gift. Under the old dispensation the Spirit had been granted sporadically to individuals and even that seems to have stopped in the latter centuries. At Pentecost the Spirit is poured out on the whole Church and, according to the prophecy of Joel, is given even to the women and the slaves. This is the striking feature of the new age. Everyone who repents and is baptized will receive the Spirit. When the Spirit is absent from any community it is a cause for astonishment (Acts 8.16; 19.2). That each of the baptized possesses the Spirit in a way which is perceptible is taken for granted (Acts 15.8; 9.17; 10.44; 11.16; 19.6); it is a normal consequence of coming to faith. Unlike Paul, however, Luke does not see the Spirit as totally shaping the life of the believer, still less as constituting his very existence as a Christian. He still regards the Spirit as a force from outside, unpredictable and inscrutable, but it provides for each community the power to execute its missionary task.

The two passages of Acts, which are most often referred to in connection with confirmation, must be read with this distinctive theology in mind. The first of these is the story of the conversion of the Samaritans (8.4-18). In 1.8 Christ says to the disciples: 'You shall receive power when the Holy Spirit has come upon you; and you shall be my witnesses in Jerusalem and in all Judea and Samaria and to the ends of the earth.' Jerusalem remains the scene of the first seven chapters, but the bitter persecution brought on by Stephen and the Hellenists causes a dispersion, and thus Philip, one of the seven 'deacons', goes to Samaria to preach the word. This was a momentous step because of the mutual hatred between Jews and Samaritans. Philip's preaching was successful. Many believers were baptized including the magician, Simon.

> Now when the apostles at Jerusalem heard that Samaria had received the word of God, they sent to them Simon and John, who came down and prayed for them that they might receive the Holy Spirit; for it had not yet fallen on any of them, but they had only been baptized in the name of the Lord Jesus. Then they laid their hands on them and they received the Holy Spirit (8.14-17).

The first thing we are told here is that when the extraordinary news that some Samaritans had believed the Gospel reached Jerusalem, the apostles sent two representatives. Luke's intention here is to point out that, at this first enlarging of the field of mission, the apostles were careful to establish personal contact and thus maintain the unity of the Church. Similarly when Jerusalem hears that the word has been preached in gentile Antioch they send Barnabas to make the contact. Paul, after his conversion, goes himself to contact the apostles at Jerusalem. Luke, therefore, is concerned to point out that at every stage a link with the Jerusalem church and with the apostles is established.

When Peter and John arrive in Samaria, they find to their surprise that this new community has not received the Spirit: 'for it had not yet fallen on any of them.' In the terms of Pauline theology this statement would mean that these people were not yet Christians and imply that their conversion was in some way defective. But for Luke faith, conversion, and being a Christian are not the work of the Holy Spirit. What this community lacks is the Spirit of prophecy which will enable it to spread the Gospel in its turn and consolidate the faith in Samaria. Even so the lack is remarkable.

In later ages preoccupation with Church order has led many to think that the Samaritans did not receive the Spirit because Philip, being only a deacon, was not empowered to give it. But this does not seem to have been Luke's intention, for the same Stephen later baptizes an Egyptian eunuch and nothing is said about the Spirit being withheld – the secondary Western text even affirms that the Spirit fell on him (Acts 8.38-39). Paul receives the Spirit when he is baptized by Ananias who was not an apostle (9.17-19).

Luke does not tell us why the Spirit did not come upon the Samaritans; he recognises that the Spirit is unpredictable. What we are meant to notice is that in this new outpost of the expanding mission, the prophetic Spirit, which is the divine power sustaining the work of evangelization, descends only when contact with the Jerusalem church is established. On the other hand the point of the Simon Magus episode is the mistake of thinking that the Holy Spirit is a force which can be given and manipulated at will by any

91

man. St Augustine saw this very clearly: 'The Spirit testified in this way lest men should arrogate to themselves what belongs to God' (*Serm.* 266,3-6; 267).

The passage concerning the disciples of the Baptist at Ephesus (19.1-7) poses many difficulties. It forms one side as it were of a diptych with the story of Apollos (18.24-28), who though knowing only the baptism of John, was nevertheless 'fervent in the Spirit', 'spoke and taught accurately the things concerning Jesus' and displays that boldness in defending the Gospel which finally won for Paul the recognition of the apostles (9.27). This man is accepted among Christians without any mention being made of his baptism. It seems that Luke wishes to portray him as one on whom the Spirit has descended of his own accord, thus making a Christian of him. In contrast to Apollos the group at Ephesus confess that they have never even heard that there is a Holy Spirit. Paul then enlightens them about the baptism of John and faith in Jesus.

> On hearing this they were baptized in the name of the Lord Jesus. And when Paul had laid his hands upon them, the Holy Spirit came on them and they spoke with tongues and prophesied (19.5-6).

Linking this passage with 8.17, many over the centuries have thought that the normal rite of Christian initiation in the time of Luke consisted of baptism followed by the imposition of an apostle's hands for the imparting of the Spirit. Both of these passages, however, seem to refer to the exception rather than the norm, and nowhere else is mention made of a regular laying on of hands for the reception of the Spirit after baptism.

Why, therefore, does Paul not only baptize but also lay hands on these men? There seems to be no entirely satisfactory answer to this question. Perhaps we are meant to recognise that Paul's function with regard to this group at Ephesus was similar to that of Peter and John in Samaria. The new community in Samaria remained without the Spirit until communion with Jerusalem was established. The strange company at Ephesus are clearly distinguished from ordinary Jews and pagans, but they existed without any knowledge of the Spirit. Through Paul they are joined to the Church by Christian baptism. Perhaps he makes a special point of praying and laying hands on them that they may receive the Spirit, precisely because they had lived all this time without any knowledge of him.

The Acts of the Apostles do not, therefore, provide any evidence that in apostolic times there was regularly any special rite other than baptism for the imparting of the Holy Spirit. Indeed the very idea that the gift of the Holy Spirit might be tied to a rite of hand-laying is alien from Luke's way of thinking. The Holy Spirit is independent even of baptism. Once he comes on men before baptism (10.44), once without it (2.1-4) and once on a man who knows only John's baptism (18.25). Luke is concerned to emphasize the freedom of the Spirit. He is not given by any man, and if any human activity can be said to influence his coming it is only that of prayer and a gesture indicative of prayer.

Yet the laying on of hands with prayer for the outpouring of the Spirit may have been a more frequent accompaniment of baptism, at least in some circles, than Luke gives one to think. The author of the Epistle to the Hebrews mentions it in connection with elementary doctrine:

> Therefore let us leave the elementary doctrines of Christ and go on to maturity, not laying again the foundations of repentance from dead works and of faith towards God, with instructions about ablutions, the laying on of hands, the resurrection of the dead and eternal judgment... (6.1-2).

Most commentators agree that this may refer to part of the initiation ceremony, but the passage does not permit any very certain interpretation. There are no other texts in the New Testament to guide us. We can therefore only speculate as to how the post-baptismal rites attested in the early third century may have grown up. It is not unlikely that, as the visible manifestations of the Spirit's presence became a less frequent accompaniment of baptism, the need was felt in some churches to pray over the neophytes according to the model provided in Acts 8.17 and 19.6.

In the Fourth Gospel the Spirit is conceived in terms much closer to those of Paul than to those of Luke. The continued delay of the *Parousia* and the death of the first generation of Christians led John to reinterpret the message so as to emphasize more than Paul the presence even now of the promised salvation. To this end the Hellenistic under-standing of the Spirit as heavenly substance is once again adopted. But in John there is a far more thorough-going elimination of the older ideas concerning the Spirit than in Paul. There is no thought in his work of sporadic coming of the Spirit, the extraordinary nature of manifestations, ecstatic phenomena or miraculous acts. Jesus is not presented as one 'possessed' by the Spirit; his inspired speech and his miracles are nowhere attributed to the Spirit. John wishes to show that the Father himself and not just the gift of the Father, is genuinely encountered in the Christ-event. Therefore he completely abandons the idea of inspiration because this emphasizes the distinction between God and Jesus. He understands the Spirit as that by which the distinction is overcome.

The Spirit is given only after Christ's exaltation in death and resurrection and it is the direct result of this exaltation. For this reason John does not mention the delay of ten days described by Luke, but depicts the giving of the Spirit as the first act of the risen Christ (20.20). The function of the Paraclete is to make the divine reality present as it was present in Jesus and will continue to be present in his word. The Paraclete is the spirit of truth in the midst of the world of unreality and mere appearance; in this sense the spirit is the antithesis of the 'flesh'. Jesus came in the flesh, and because of this it was possible to see him and yet not to see him, to

94

hear him and yet not to hear him (6.36; 5.37f.). This even applied, in a certain sense, to those who were his own so long as he was with them (14.5-11). In this sense the historical Jesus as such is the 'flesh' which profits nothing (6.63): only the Spirit, which comes to the community in the Word, gives life. Only the 'Spirit of truth' genuinely discloses Jesus to the disciples (14.26; 16.13) and thus glorifies him (16.13). The words of the historical Jesus only take on life-giving force when they become the words of the Spirit (16.8-11). These words of the Spirit are those spoken in the authoritative proclamation of his community (20.22f.; 15.26f.).

For the Christian 'to be born of the Spirit', 'to be born from above' or 'from God', is contrasted with being born 'from below', 'from the devil', 'from the world'; to be born of the Spirit is the opposite of being born from the flesh (3.1-15). The man who is born of the Spirit belongs to the other world, he is like the wind that blows where it wills; of his whence and whither the world knows nothing, because the Spirit is a life-giving power which makes the one who is born of the Spirit belong to the divine sphere. But the Spirit is that which arouses faith. Rebirth by water and the Holy Spirit is therefore parallel to the insistence on faith and baptism in other writers. A man enters the new life through the water of baptism and the faith in the word which is produced by the Spirit. Very close to this notion in John's Gospel is the idea of the anointing of the Christian in the First Epistle of John (2.26-27). This is the action of God who through the Spirit arouses faith and maintains it.

John has taken the old idea of the Spirit of prophecy and stripped it of much of its ecstatic and intermittent nature. What remains is no longer so much a phenomenon, but the power of God which is present in the preaching of the community, the power to preach Jesus as redeemer through which the divine word encounters man. The Spirit shapes the life of the people of God and in so doing summons and judges the world.

95

The Apocalypse contains yet another distinctive conception of the Spirit, which in certain ways is unique in the New Testament. The idea of the Spirit of prophecy is dominant again (10.19), but it is related to a special state of consciousness designated by the words 'in the Spirit' (1.10; 4.2). The Spirit is the power which gives visions the ordinary man cannot have. It leads a man off into wonderful regions which the natural man does not perceive (17.3; 21.10). The Spirit speaks recalling the promises of Scripture and formulating them afresh (14.13). He is experienced as deity so far transcending everything human, that the human speaker can fade from the scene altogether (2.17; 14.13; 22.17). Yet the Spirit always addresses himself to the community as such; the one through whom he speaks is of little importance.

The words of the risen Christ are also the words which the Spirit speaks to the churches (2.1 cf. 7; 2.8 cf. 11 etc.). Thus, in the Spirit, Christ is with his own, yet when the community calls to the Lord in heaven, 'The Spirit and the Bride say: Come' (22.17). When the community calls for its Lord, it does so in the power of the Spirit.

2. The Church's Understanding of the Scriptural Data

It would be far too simple to consider that these different conceptions of the Holy Spirit could be arranged to show an evolution in which each stage represents an advance on what preceded it, so that, for example, we would be justified in rejecting the thought of Luke for that of Paul or both for that of John. The Catholic must treat every element in the New Testament with all the respect which attaches to it. It was necessary for the Church in this matter to retain the valuable insights of Luke and the Apocalypse along with the teaching of Paul and John. What we have seen in the writings of the Fathers concerning the gift of the Spirit in

Christian initiation shows that in various places and different epochs the proportion of the elements selected from the various scriptural sources has varied in accordance with the current understanding of the work of the Spirit in the Church.

What has been called the Antiochene rite of initiation bears witness to the lasting influence of Paul's teaching in an area where so many of the churches were founded by him. The gift of the Spirit was not thought of as being in any way additional to baptismal regeneration, but rather its formal cause. The anointing before baptism is surely an attempt to give visible expression to the Pauline and Johannine idea of the spiritual anointing, the power of God which arouses and sustains human faith. In this sense Ephraem and Theodoret are right to see it as the sign of the gift of the Spirit. Those who like Chrysostom insist that the advent of the Spirit is simultaneous with the baptismal participation in the death and resurrection of Christ, are influenced by Pauline doctrine almost to the exclusion of Lucan insights. Thus Chrysostom is unable to admit that the Samaritans in Acts 9 have not received the Holy Spirit at their baptism by Philip: 'How, you will ask, have these people not received the Spirit? They have received the Spirit of remission, but the Spirit of signs they have not yet received' (*In Act. Hom.* 18,2). He can only understand the gift of the Spirit in Luke as a charismatic gift additional to the principal gift of the Spirit in baptismal rebirth.

The writings of Luke, however, seem to have had a much deeper influence on the early baptismal rites of the West. In the rite of Hippolytus the gift of the Holy Spirit is not directly connected with the baptismal regeneration as such. It is spoken of as that which makes it possible to serve God according to his will and is only invoked once the baptismal act is over. A similar doctrine and practice is found in Tertullian who is the more interesting because he refrains from connecting the descent of the Spirit at the laying on of the bishop's hand with the charismatic gifts which he urges the neophytes to pray for privately after the ceremony.

Irenaeus used 1 Cor 12.13 to establish a distinction between two functions of the Spirit: by the first, existence is given to the new creature in Christ; by the second, this new life is nourished and grows. The second of these functions he connects closely with the Old Testament concept of the Spirit of prophecy, 'being watered whereby a man bears fruit of life to God' (*Demonstr.* 99). Like Paul, Irenaeus expects the Spirit-given life of the Church, if not of the individual, to be manifest in extraordinary charismatic activity. He goes so far as to say that those who, out of fear of false prophets, deny the existence of prophetic gifts in the Church, are guilty of the unforgiveable sin against the Holy Spirit (*Adv. Haer.* III, II, 12; *Demonstr.* 99). His insistence on the Spirit of prophecy shows how seriously Irenaeus takes the Lucan doctrine that the Church is endowed with a special outpouring of the Spirit for the promulgation of the Gospel, which cannot be simply reduced to personal rebirth into the new heavenly existence and a consequent life in the Spirit.

Cyprian uses the same distinction between the two activities of the Holy Spirit to differentiate the effects of the hand-laying from those of baptism, but he makes no reference to charismatic gifts. From this time onwards Western writers reserve the phrases 'gift of the Spirit', 'reception of the Spirit' (in the Lucan sense) to designate the bestowal of something additional to baptismal regeneration. Augustine follows in the same line of thought, but gives it a much more Pauline twist by interpreting this gift of the Spirit in function of Romans 5.5; the gift of the Spirit means growth in charity. He recognises that it is possible to have charity, and therefore to have the Spirit, yet not to possess him in the way the Lord had promised that Christians would possess him. To possess him in this way is to possess him as Paraclete, and it is characterized, not by charismatic activity, but by the seven gifts listed in Isaiah. Here the perspective is more Johannine than Pauline.

From the end of the fourth century a clear distinction is made in the West between the baptismal rebirth from water and the Holy Spirit, and the reception of the Paraclete or sevenfold Spirit through hand-laying or chrismation. The same distinction was gradually accepted in the East. The imbalance of this doctrine was that the Lucan emphasis on the pouring out of the prophetic Spirit for the spreading of the Gospel gives way to one on the spiritual growth of the individual and the personal struggles of the Christian life. No doubt this development was made the easier because the charismatic gifts had become rare, and this may not be unconnected with the growing tendency of the Church to find its security in institutional structures.

The confirmation doctrine of the mediaeval West, which stemmed from the Carolingian theologians, in contrast, placed all its emphasis on the gift of strength to confess the faith before the world. In Thomas Aquinas this tendency reached its logical conclusion; the grace of confirmation was distinguished from those of baptism precisely in so far as it was ordered to the exterior needs of the Church and the Gospel and not to the interior growth of the individual. Here we have something which looks at first like a return to the Lucan concept of the Spirit. But there is no emphasis on the charismatic nature of the gift. The emphasis on strength for the fight to the exclusion of the other six gifts of the Spirit made it appear that there was an enormous difference between the grace of confirmation and the outpouring of the Spirit at Pentecost.

In view of all that has been said, it seems clear that, for a complete account of the New Testament doctrine of the fulfilment of God's promises concerning the Spirit, it is necessary, even when the Pauline theology is accepted as the basic model, to speak of a special outpouring of the Holy Spirit upon the Church and upon each Christian, whereby power is received from on high for the task of spreading the Gospel message. The Catholic Church and all the churches of the East recognise the second part of the rite of Christian initiation as the sacrament of this outpouring.

3. The Institution of the Sacrament

The institution of such a sacrament by Christ need no longer be a problem. Thomas Aquinas said long ago that Christ instituted this sacrament not by demonstrating any rite but by promising to send the Holy Spirit. We have seen that this sending of the Spirit implies more than the remission of sins, new birth and new supernatural existence, it implies a nourishing, a leading, a guiding by the Spirit of God which invests the Christian with power from on high and is capable of taking him out of himself in the service of the Gospel. Relying on Christ's promise, the Church has been wont to pray that each new member may possess the promised Paraclete in this way. To this extent the sacrament of confirmation is similar to the sacrament by which the Church ordains its ministers. Both rites are essentially a prayer for the fulfilment of a promise, a prayer made with the assurance that it will be heard. The various rites and indicative words which have been used over the ages in the administration of this sacrament, are the proclamation that the prayer of the Church is heard and that the promise is fulfilled for certain individuals.

4. The Effect of the Sacrament

The fundamental belief behind the Church's practice of chrismation or confirmation is well expressed by Faustus of Riez in reference to Pentecost: 'What the imposition of hands bestows upon each at the confirmation of the neophytes, the descent of the Holy Spirit at that time conferred upon all the assembly of the faithful.' As described by Luke the Pentecost-event was specially orientated towards the growth of the Church and the spreading of the faith, yet it is clear from John and from Paul that it also has an interior dimension in so far as the life of the individual Christian is guided and grows under the influence of the Holy Spirit. The sacrament of confirmation, therefore, is the sacrament of the mysterious influence of the Paraclete upon the life of each Christian enabling him to bear witness to Christ. The extent of this influence will fluctuate in accordance with the receptiveness of the individual. The Holy Spirit bestows his gifts dividing to each as he wills, but they will be received only in so far as the individual is ready to receive them. This applies not only to the gifts of faith, charity, prayer, knowledge and insight, but also to the more spectacular charisms. Baptism for the adult should normally be the expression of a profound conversion, a complete dedication to the Lord and a point of great religious tension. At such a moment the believer is especially receptive to the Spirit. Little wonder, therefore, that the neophytes of the early Church frequently broke into charismatic utterance, and gave other evidence of the activity of the Spirit with them for the edification of the Church. When baptism is conferred in infancy and confirmation received in due course at a time when there may as yet be little personal conversion towards Christ, receptivity to the Spirit will be low. This does not empty the sacrament either of meaning or of effect; it remains the proclamation of the mystery of Pentecost in the life of the candidates. But the Spirit will only gradually be able to dominate their lives, and only gradually will they open themselves to receive his gifts. Later turning-points in their lives may seem much more Pentecostal than was their reception of the sacrament of confirmation. Yet these moments as well as all the graces of prayer and understanding, of growth in virtue, or in ability to love, the deepening of peace within themselves, and developing ability to help others to believe, all these, not to mention the more obviously miraculous gifts and ecstatic powers, will be but the manifestation of that outpouring of the Spirit which the faith of the Church proclaimed over them at their confirmation. This indwelling of the Holy Spirit with the resulting activity of the 'life in the Spirit' is in St Paul's sense the seal of God on the faith of the believer – a faith which itself proceeds from the Spirit. It is anointing which equips the Christian with power from on high through which the Gospel message is spread and the people of God is built up.

5. The Character of Confirmation

Like baptism and orders, confirmation is a sacrament which is only conferred once. It is the proclamation in faith by the Church that the promised Spirit has been poured out on certain individuals. This is an act of Christ and his Church which is true in itself and need never be repeated. The candidate is marked, as it were, by the ceremony, and remains a man who has been confirmed. The effect of the sacrament may be completely blocked by his lack of faith or sinful disposition, yet he remains one over whom the Church has prayed and proclaimed the outpouring of the Holy Spirit. As soon as the blocks to this grace from his side are removed, the action of Christ in the sacrament will take effect. This is what the Council of Trent meant when it declared that this sacrament confers a character or mark (Dz 1609). Thomas Aquinas had already developed this idea further by saying that the character of confirmation was a deputing of the candidate by Christ to serve him in spiritual combat against the enemies of the faith. On the general idea of 'character' and its development the reader is referred to *The Theology of the Sacraments* in this series.

6. The Minister of Confirmation

The ancient Roman tradition which insisted that the bishop alone might administer this sacrament, though less well founded upon the text of Acts than has frequently been claimed, preserves a very important aspect of Luke's doctrine about the gift of the Spirit. The Spirit is given to the Church for the accomplishment of its mission. As the word spreads to Judea, to Samaria and to the gentile world, Luke is careful to stress the link which was maintained with the church at Jerusalem. The bishop is the symbol of unity in the local church and its point of communion with the other local churches throughout the world. The preface to the new Order of Confirmation says that the bishop should usually administer the sacrament himself, because in this way the link which joins those confirmed to the Church is more clearly shown as well as the mandate received from Christ to bear witness among men. The bishops are the successors of the Apostles who themselves gave the Holy Spirit by the laying on of hands precisely so that this unity might be maintained.

Happily the mediaeval laws which exaggerated this principle into the theory of a power given to the bishops alone have now been revoked. These laws were largely responsible for the separation of confirmation from baptism, and for many misunderstandings concerning it.

7. The Age for the Confirmation of those Baptized in Infancy

Traditionally and theologically confirmation belongs with baptism as a part of the ceremony of Christian initiation. If baptism may be given to infants there is no special reason why confirmation cannot also be conferred on them. This is the practice of the Eastern churches and it has been shown that the custom of deferring confirmation to about

103

the age of seven in the West is one that grew up by accident rather than by any theological design. In comparatively recent times there have been attempts to make the reception of confirmation a moment at which the young person makes a dramatic ratification of the baptismal promises, thus turning the sacrament into one of commitment, if not into some form of puberty rite. If confirmation is to be regarded in this way, obviously it is better to delay it until the personal commitment of the candidate can be given unhampered by any pressures from the family or from the school, and twenty would be a better age than seven.

There can be no doubt that, at the present time, the defection from the Church of young people, who have been baptized as infants and are supposed to have received a Christian education, is very general. In such circumstances those who do not wish to defect feel the need to make some public act of commitment. It must be realized, however, that confirmation is not and has never been a sacrament of commitment: it is the sacrament of the mystery of Pentecost in the life of one who in conversion and baptism has committed himself to Christ and is reborn to a new existence. The pastoral problem which the Church must face in this matter is not the question of the age most suitable for confirmation, but that of the expediency of infant baptism in an age when the methods of Christian education seem to provide little protection for the growth of the divine life received through that sacrament. Ideally the one baptized in infancy should grow in grace as the capacity for truly human activity develops. As he comes to the age of reason he should discover himself as believing of his own free choice – for one cannot believe in any other way. He should have no need to experience the drama of a conversion by which he rejects a defective way of life and turns to Christ. If such a grace-given development is to take place, however, the child needs not only to be reborn by baptism, but also to be given to drink by the working of the Holy Spirit at least as soon as he comes to the age of reason.

The Church has always recognised that the sacraments of baptism and confirmation can do little for a child if the environment in which it is brought up is not favourable to the growth of faith. For this reason the indiscriminate baptism of the children of non-Christian parents has never been allowed. If the society in which we now live is inimical to the growth of infant faith, we must surely question the expediency of infant baptism rather than try to twist the sacrament of confirmation into a second sacrament of commitment.

APPENDIX

CONFIRMATION WITHIN MASS

Order for the conferring of Confirmation during Mass. An official translation made from *Ordo Confirmationis*, Vatican 1971.

The Liturgy of the Word is carried out in the ordinary way. The readings, however, may be taken either entirely or in part either from the Mass of the day or from the texts provided in the Lectionary.

After the Gospel, the Bishop (and priests who are to assist him) sit in the places prepared. Those to be confirmed are presented by the parish priest or by another priest or deacon, or even a catechist, according to the custom of the place, in the following way: Each candidate, if possible, should be called by name and then come to the sanctuary. If they are children, they should be led by a sponsor or parent and stand together before the celebrant. If there are many, their names are not called. They take their place at the appropriate time before the Bishop.

HOMILY OR ADDRESS

Then the Bishop gives a brief Homily. Its purpose is to lead the candidates and their sponsors, parents and the whole body of the faithful to a deeper understanding of the mystery of Confirmation, developing the themes of the readings.

This can be done as follows or in similar words:
We read in the Acts of the Apostles how the apostles, in

fulfilment of the Lord's promise, received the Holy Spirit and had the power to complete the sacrament of Baptism by the Holy Spirit's gift. When St Paul imposed his hands on those who had already been baptised, the Holy Spirit came down upon them and they spoke with tongues and prophesied.

The Bishops, who are the successors of the apostles, enjoy the same power and (either directly, or indirectly through those priests lawfully designated to perform this ministry) give the Holy Spirit to those already renewed by Baptism.

In our own day the coming of the Holy Spirit is not signalised by the gift of tongues. All the same our faith tells us that he who diffuses God's love in our hearts and gathers us together in the oneness of faith and diversity of calling assuredly comes to us and acts invisibly to build up the holiness and unity of His Church.

Dearly beloved, you are about to receive the gift of the Holy Spirit which is for you a spiritual marking, uniting you more closely with Christ and making you more perfect members of his Church. Christ himself, anointed by the Holy Spirit when John baptised him, was sent forth to the work of his ministry which was the enkindling on earth of the flame of that same Holy Spirit.

You who have already been baptised will now receive the power of his Spirit and the sign of his cross on your foreheads. You must therefore bear witness to his passion and resurrection before the world and your life must proclaim everywhere, as the apostle tells us, the sweet odour of Christ. His mystical body, the Church, the people of God, receives different gifts from him which the same Holy Spirit apportions to each and all for the upbuilding of this Body in oneness and love.

With the Holy Spirit as your guide you are then to be living members of this Church, zealous in the service of all men like Christ himself who came not to be ministered to but to minister.

And now, before you receive the Spirit, you should call to mind the faith which you acknowledged in Baptism or which your parents or god-parents acknowledged on your behalf together with the whole Church.

RENEWAL OF BAPTISMAL PROMISES

Then the Bishop questions the candidates all standing together saying:
Do you reject Satan and all his works and empty promises?
The candidates all reply together:
I do.
Bishop:
Do you believe in God, the Father almighty, creator of heaven and earth?
Confirmandi:
I do.
Bishop:
Do you believe in Jesus Christ, his only Son, our Lord, who was born of the Virgin Mary, was crucified, died, and was buried, rose from the dead, and is now seated at the right hand of the Father?
Confirmandi:
I do.
Bishop:
Do you believe in the Holy Spirit, the Lord and giver of life, who today, through the Sacrament of Confirmation will be given to you in a special way, as he was to the apostles on the day of Pentecost?
Confirmandi:
I do.
Bishop:
Do you believe in the holy Catholic Church, the communion of saints, the forgiveness of sins, the resurrection of the body and life everlasting?

Confirmandi:
I do.
The Bishop accepts this profession, proclaiming the Church's faith:
This is our faith. This is the faith of the Church in Christ Jesus Our Lord which we are proud to profess.

All the faithful assent by answering:
Amen.

It is permitted, if thought desirable, to substitute some other formula for This is our faith... *or even a suitable hymn wherein the community can express its faith with united voice.*

IMPOSITION OF HANDS

Then the Bishop (together with the priests assisting him) stands with joined hands, facing the people, and says:
Dearly beloved:
Let us ask God the Father Almighty
of his great love
to pour out his Holy Spirit
on these his adopted children
who have already been renewed
by the baptism of everlasting life.
May they be strengthened with the fulness of his gifts,
and by his anointing
be made more like to Christ, the Son of God.

All then pray in silence for a while.

The Bishop (and the priests assisting him) impose their hands over the confirmandi. The Bishop alone says:
Almighty God,

Father of our Lord Jesus Christ,
you have given new life
to these children of yours
by water and the Holy Spirit,
freeing them from their sins.
Now, O Lord
send down upon them
the Holy Spirit the comforter;
give them the spirit of wisdom and understanding.
the spirit of counsel and fortitude,
the spirit of knowledge and devotion.
Fill them with the spirit of fear of yourself.
Through Christ our Lord.
R/ Amen.

ANOINTING WITH CHRISM

The deacon then offers the holy chrism to the Bishop. Each of the confirmands advances to the Bishop, or if it is more convenient, the Bishop goes to them. The Sponsor places the right hand on the confirmand's shoulder and tells the Bishop the name to be taken. Or the confirmand himself may tell the Bishop the name.

The Bishop dips his right thumb in the chrism and traces the sign of the cross on the forehead of the confirmand, saying:
N. Receive the seal of the gift of the Holy Spirit.

The confirmand replies:
Amen.
The Bishop adds:
Peace be with you.
The confirmand answers:
And also with you.

If priests assist the Bishop in conferring the Sacrament, all the vessels containing the holy chrism are brought by the deacon or servers to the Bishop who gives one to each of the priests who come forward to him.

The confirmands approach the Bishop or the priests. Alternatively, the Bishop or priests go to the confirmands. They are anointed in the manner already described.

During the anointing any suitable hymns may be sung. After the anointing the Bishop (and priests) cleanse their hands.

THE BIDDING PRAYER

The Bidding Prayer follows either in the form below or a similar one authorised by the competent authority:

Bishop:
Dearly beloved, let us humbly ask God the Almighty Father that we may pray with one mind; just as by the gift of the Holy Spirit we are one in faith and hope and love.

Deacon or Minister:
May those who have been strengthened by the gift of the Holy Spirit, have their faith deepened and their charity increased, so that they may bear witness by their love to Christ our Lord.
Lord, hear us. R/ Lord, graciously hear us.

Deacon or Minister:
May their parents and god-parents do all in their power, by word and example, to lead those whom they have sponsored in the faith to follow in Christ's footsteps.
Lord hear us. R/ Lord, graciously hear us.

Deacon or Minister:

May God's Holy Church, united with our Holy Father Pope N., our Bishop N. and all the Bishops, gathered together by the Holy Spirit in the oneness of faith and love, grow and spread continually until the Lord's coming.
Lord, hear us. R/ Lord, graciously hear us.

Deacon or Minister:
May all the peoples of the world, who share the same Creator and Father, look on each other as brothers, regardless of race or nationality, and seek God's kingdom, a kingdom of peace and joy in the Holy Spirit, with true dedication.
Lord, hear us. R/ Lord, graciously hear us.

Deacon or Minister:
Let us commend ourselves and all God's people, living and dead, to the intercession of our Blessed Lady, the holy and immaculate Virgin Mother of God.
Hail Mary, &c.

Deacon or Minister:
Let us now pray for a while in silence.

Then the Bishop says:
O God, you gave the Holy Spirit to your apostles. It was your will also that through them and their successors he should be given to the rest of the faithful. Listen to our prayer and grant that just as at the beginning of the Church's life many wonderful things took place; so now the hearts of all believers may be uplifted. Through Christ our Lord. R/ Amen.

THE EUCHARISTIC LITURGY

When the Bidding Prayer has been said, the Eucharistic Liturgy follows according to the Order of Mass, apart from the following:

(a) The Creed is omitted because the profession of faith has already been made.

(b) Some of those confirmed should join in the Offertory procession.

(c) When the Roman Canon is used, the proper Hanc Igitur *is said.*

Adults who have been confirmed, and, if it is thought suitable, their sponsors, parents, husbands and wives, and catechists, may receive Holy Communion under both kinds.

THE BLESSING

In place of the usual blessing at the end of Mass, the following blessing may be given or the following Prayer over the People.

May God the Almighty Father
who has renewed you by water and the Holy Spirit
and made you his children by adoption,
bless you,
and may he keep you worthy of his fatherly love.
R/ Amen.
May his only-begotten Son
who promised that the spirit of truth
would remain with his Church,
bless you,
and may he by his power strengthen you
to proclaim the true faith. R/ Amen.

May the Holy Spirit
who enkindled the fire of love in the hearts of his disciples

113

bless you,
and may he lead you, united together,
safely into the joy of God's kingdom. R/ Amen.

Immediately he adds:

May Almighty God bless you, the Father,
the Son, ✠ and the Holy Spirit.

Instead of the form of blessing given above, the Prayer over the People may be said.

PRAYER OVER THE PEOPLE

The deacon or minister gives the invitation, saying: Bow down for the Blessing, *or some other form.*

Then the Bishop with his hands extended over the people says:

Confirm, O God, what you have wrought in us
and preserve the gifts of the Holy Spirit
in the hearts of your faithful people.
May they not be ashamed
to acknowledge before the world Christ crucified
and carry out his commands
with dedication and love:
through Christ our Lord.
R/ Amen.

He adds immediately:
May Almighty God bless you, the Father,
the Son ✠ and the Holy Spirit.
R/ Amen.

TABLES

Didascalia Apostolorum (*ed. R. H. Connolly, p. 146, see above p. 12*) *Written 200–225*	Catechetical Instructions of John Chrysostom (*conveniently collected in translation by P. W. Harkins, Ancient Christian Writers 31*). *Delivered at Antioch c. 388 and 390*	Catechetical Instructions of Theodore of Mopsuestia (*extracts from Mingana's translation in Whitaker pp. 36–42*). *Delivered between 392 and 428*
	On the Friday or Saturday before the Easter Vigil Renunciation of Satan and attachment to Christ (p. 49–51)	*At the Vigil of Easter* Renunciation of Satan and attachment to Christ with confession of faith
Anointing of the head by the bishop with imposition of his hand	Anointing with myron and signing by the bishop with the formula: 'N. is anointed in the name of the Father' etc. (p. 51–2, cf. p. 169)	Signing on the forehead by the bishop (who wears a splendid vestment) with oil of anointing. Formula: 'N. is anointed in the name of the Father' etc. Sponsors put a strip of linen round the head of the candidate (Serm. 3, p. 39)
Total anointing, which for a woman is done by a deaconess	*During the Vigil* Undressing and total anointing (p. 52, cf. p. 169)	Undressing. Total anointing by minister (Serm. 3, p. 40) Blessing of the Water
Baptism with invocation of the divine names by the bishop, priest or deacon	Triple immersion with the formula: 'N. is baptized in the name of the Father' etc. while the bishop keeps his hand on the candidate's head (pp. 52, 170)	Triple immersion with the formula: 'N. is baptized in the name of the Father' etc., while the bishop imposes his hand on the candidate's head (p. 41) Clothing with a splendid garment of linen Bishop signs the candidate on the forehead (with oil?) using the formula: 'N. is signed in the name of the Father' etc.(*ibid.* p. 41)

Sermon of Proclus of Constantinople (*see Harkins p. 228 = translation of extract from unedited MS given by Wenger, S.C. 50, p. 100*) 426–446	Homilies of Narsai (?) (*translation of R. H. Connolly reproduced in Whitaker pp. 42–48*). Between 437 & 503	Apostolic Constitutions VII (*translation in Whitaker pp. 29–31*). Compiled about 400
Raising of hands Anointing with myron	Renunciation of Satan and confession of faith (Hom. 22, p. 42–3) Marking of the seal on the forehead with the formula: 'N. is signed in the name of the Father' etc. (44–46)	Renunciation of Satan and profession of faith (c. 41) Anointing with oil blessed by the priest for the remission of sins, the first preparation for baptism so that he may become worthy of initiation (c. 42)
Making brilliant with oil	Total anointing (p. 46)	Blessing and thanksgiving with epiclesis over the water.
Immersion	Blessing of the water Baptism with the formula: 'N. is baptized in the name of the Father' etc. and triple immersion (Hom. 21 pp. 46–47)	Baptism in the name of the Father etc. (c. 43)
White garment	Clothing with garments like a bridegroom (p. 47)	
Lamp	Embraced by all	Anointing with chrism and laying on of the hand with a formula which speaks of the sweet odour of Christ (c. 44)

HIPPOLYTUS, c. 213. (Botte: *La Tradition Apostolique de S. Hippolyte*, pp. 42–57 (Whitaker p. 3)	TERTULLIAN. 193–221 (Whitaker pp. 7–9)	ST. AMBROSE. 374–397 (*De Sacramentis*; *De Mysteriis*. Ed. Botte (S.C. 25 bis), (Whitaker, pp. 117–123)
Final reunion of *electi* on the Saturday evening. Prayer on bended knee, exorcism with imposition of hand, exsufflation, anointing of forehead, ears and nostrils (XX, 7–9)		Ceremony of *effeta* on Saturday
		With touching of ears and nostrils (*De Sac.* I, 2–3)
	Renunciation of the Devil and the world under the bishop's hand (*De Corona*, 3)	
VIGIL Prayer over the water at cockcrow (XXI, 1) Undressing (XXI, 3) Thanksgiving over some oil, exorcism over other oil (XXI, 6)	VIGIL Prayer for sanctification of the water (*De Bapt.* 4)	VIGIL
		Anointing as athlete of Christ (*De Sac.* I, 4)
Renunciation of Satan (XXI, 9)	Renunciation repeated (*De Corona*, 3)	Renunciation of Satan and world (*De Sac.* I, 5)
Anointing with oil of exorcism (XXI, 10)		Exorcism and consecration of the water (*De Sac.* II, 20)
Triple immersion with credal interrogation (XXI, 11–18). Administered by bishop or presbyter	Triple immersion accompanied by 'a little more than our Lord says in the Gospel' (*De Corona*, 3)	Triple immersion with credal interrogation (*De Sac.* II, 20; *De Myst.* 28)

GELASIAN SACRAMENTARY, 6th c. Book I, xlii–xliv (Whitaker pp. 173–178)	*ORDO ROMANUS IX*, 7th c. (Whitaker pp. 192–194)	*PONTIFICAL OF ROMAN CURIA* 13th c. (Andrieu, *Le Pontifical.* I p. 241–2) XXXII 13–33
Early Saturday morning, exorcism of infants with hand-laying Nostrils & ears touched with spittle, formula: *effeta* (70–71) Anointing of breast and back	Saturday, third hour, exorcism with hand-laying, signing by presbyter Nostrils & ears touched with spittle, formula: *effeta* etc. Anointing of breast and back (85–87)	Saturday morning while 'vigil' is in progress exorcism by presbyter signing Nostrils & ears touched with spittle, formula: *effeta* Anointing of breast & back
Renunciation of Satan (72) Creed, prayer kneeling (72–5)	Creed, prayer kneeling (86)	After renunciation Creed, Lord's prayer (13–20)
VIGIL Consecration of the font (89)	VIGIL Consecration of the font (93–4)	Consecration of the font (21–23)
[Nakedness mentioned by John the deacon]		
Triple immersion with credal interrogation (93)	Pontiff baptizes some children. Priests & deacons others (96)	Credal interrogation Triple immersion with formula: 'I baptize you in the name of the Father etc. that you may have eternal life.' (24)

HIPPOLYTUS, c. 213. (Botte: *La Tradition Apostolique de S. Hippolyte*, pp. 42–57 (Whitaker p. 3)	TERTULLIAN. 193–221 (Whitaker pp. 7–9)	ST. AMBROSE. 374–397 (*De Sacramentis; De Mysteriis.* Ed. Botte (S.C. 25 bis), (Whitaker, pp. 117–123)
Anointing by presbyter with oil of thanksgiving: 'I anoint you with oil in the name of Jesus Christ.' (XXI, 19) Reclothing and entry into the church (XXI, 20)	Anointing with blessed oil accompanied by a signing (*De Res. Carn.* 8; *De Bapt.* 7)	Anointing of the head with *myron* by presbyter (*De Sac.* III, 1; *De Myst.* 29f.) Washing of feet (*De Sac.* III, 4) Clothing with white garment (*De Myst.* 34)
Collective imposition of the bishop's hand with the prayer: 'Lord God who made these worthy...' (XXII, 1) Anointing with consecrated oil and imposition of bishop's hand: 'I anoint you with holy oil in God the Father almighty and Christ Jesus and the Holy Spirit' (XXII, 2) 'And sealing him on the forehead, he shall give him the kiss of peace: "The Lord be with you". R/ "And with your Spirit". And so he shall do to each one severally' (XXII, 3–4)	Imposition of bishop's hand with prayer invoking the Spirit (*De Bapt.* 8)	Giving of the seal with invocation of the Spirit (*De Sac.* III, 8; *De Myst.* 42)

GELASIAN SACRAMENTARY, 6th c. Book I, xlii–xliv (Whitaker pp. 173–178)	ORDO ROMANUS IX, 7th c. (Whitaker pp. 192–194)	PONTIFICAL OF ROMAN CURIA 13th c. (Andrieu: Le Pontifical. I p. 241–2) XXXII 13–33
Anointing & signing with chrism by presbyter: 'Almighty God... himself anoints you with chrism in the name of J.C.' [White garment mentioned by John the Deacon]	Presbyter signs crown of head with chrism saying: 'Almighty God' etc. (97)	Priest or bishop signs head with chrism saying: 'Peace be with you' etc. 'Almighty God' etc. Clothing with white garment & formula (27) Presentation of candle & formula (28)
'Then the sevenfold Spirit is given them by the bishop'	Pontiff on throne, stole, chasuble & chrismal cloth given to each child (99). Clothing.	Pontiff at throne
Collective imposition of his hands and prayer: 'Almighty God... send into them' etc.	He makes prayer over them, confirming them with an invocation of the sevenfold grace of the Holy Spirit.	Imposition of hands *on each* with prayer invoking the sevenfold grace of the Holy Spirit (31–32)
'Then he signs them on the forehead with chrism saying: "The sign of Christ unto life eternal." R/ "Amen." "Peace be with you." R/ "And with your spirit." '	He makes the sign of the cross on the forehead of each saying: 'In the name of the Father & of the Son & of the Holy Spirit. Peace be with you.' R/ 'Amen.' Great care must be taken that this is not neglected for by this every baptism is confirmed and justification made for the name of Christianity	He signs each on the forehead saying: 'I sign you with the sign of the cross, and I confirm you with the chrism of salvation in the name of the Father & of the Son & of the Holy Spirit.' R/ 'Amen.' 'Peace be with you.' R/ 'And with your spirit.'

INDEX

First published in the Netherlands
Made and printed by Van Boekhoven-Bosch nv, Utrecht

BIBLIOGRAPHY

E. C. Whitaker: *Documents of the Baptismal Liturgy,* S.P.C.K., London 1960. This book is a most useful companion to the present study since it gives in full many of the liturgical documents and patristic texts to which reference is made. Occasionally it is mentioned in the text, but it also contains many more of the sources cited.

E. J. Yarnold: *The Awe-Inspiring Rites of Initiation: Baptismal Homilies of the Fourth Century,* St Paul Publications, Slough 1972.

J. D. C. Fisher: *Christian Initiation in the Medieval West,* S.P.C.K., London 1965.

J. D. C. Fisher: *Christian Initiation, The Reformation Period,* S.P.C.K., London 1970.

Leonel L. Mitchell: *Baptismal Anointing,* S.P.C.K., London 1966.

Edward Schweizer & Others: Article 'Pneuma' in *Theological Dictionary of the New Testament,* edited by Gerhard Friedrich, vol. VI, pp. 332-452, Grand Rapids, 1968. This article is also available in book-form entitled *Spirit of God,* Adam & Charles Black, London 1960.

Article 'Confirmation' in *Sacramentum Mundi,* vol. 1, edited by K. Rahner, C. Ernst and K. Smith, Burns & Oates, 1968.

THEOLOGY TODAY SERIES

The titles published to date are:

FORTHCOMING TITLES